THE LIFE STORY OF

A FARM BOY FROM SASKATCHEWAN

Allan Glen "Curly" Elliott

This book was written by the author and first printed in 2016 to share with his immediate family. Due to the appreciation the book received, and interest from others requesting to read it, he made the decision to share it with you. The book depicts events in the author's life as his memory recalls, supported by references from friends and colleagues, and other publications where possible. Some names of people featured have been omitted for their privacy, others have been included to add to the historical context. Some dialogue has been recreated for your enjoyment.

It must be noted that the word "Indian" has been kept in the narrative up until the 1980s in this story for historical accuracy. While the term is no longer how our nation refers to the Indigenous peoples of Canada, it was the term used up until it was officially retired April 17, 1982. This significant date marks when the Constitution Act was passed, including numerous amendments to the British North America Act of 1867, when the British Parliament named Canada as a domestically self-governing federation on July 1, 1867. The Constitution Act included the Canadian Charter of Rights and Freedoms which established the rights of the Indigenous Peoples of Canada. This constitution in 1982 marked Canada's parliament becoming independent from the Parliament of the United Kingdom, marking the year Canada assumed rule over its own constitution and became a sovereign nation.

Forward

Allan Glen Elliott, who is best known as Curly, wrote The Life Story of a Farm Boy from Saskatchewan to carry out a longstanding Elliott family tradition of documenting one's life story to pass on to future generations. What began as a solo project, turned into a family project - one of the best outcomes of sitting down to pass on your story to share with your loved ones. Not only did Curly document his captivating life's journey but inspired some of my favourite family holiday story telling sessions supported by priceless photographs, transporting our imaginations to each moment in time. As Curly's third granddaughter, I am beyond grateful that my Grandpa completed this book to share with us, and for reasons described below, why we decided it was also a story that is important to share with you. The book is written in the first person for our family. As I read it, I can hear my Grandpa's voice and imagine our family gathered around the projector listening to the tales behind each picture in the slideshow - of the moments captured in this book. Storytelling with your family cannot be replaced by a biography, but the depth of detail found within this book brings these stories to life in such a way that you can imagine being in Curly's shoes, seeing life as he saw it through some truly unique and monumental experiences. I hope you enjoy picturing each of these moments in Curly's life as much as I do.

Beyond serving as a vessel to document part of the Elliott clan and family's story, The Life Story of a Farm Boy from Saskatchewan captures important moments in Canadian history. Starting from humble beginnings during the Great Depression in 1928, rural Saskatchewan, Curly illustrates what life was like for many Canadians living in the prairies cultivating the farmlands that feed our country. Throughout his adventurous life, we are taken through what it was like to serve as a young RCMP (Royal Canadian Mounted Police) officer in northern Alberta, the gradual pull towards life in the big city of Calgary, and a glimpse into the brotherhood of the Freemasons. From moments travelling alone through the blistering cold wilderness for days on RCMP duties, we experience surviving in conditions not for the faint of heart, through the value of building a family, community, and working together. This is a story of adventure, resilience, courage and pride that we can all take inspiration from. In this pivotal point in our world history, we are more aware than ever about the disparity of representation in Canadian history that is widely taught. Canada has a global reputation for celebrating our diversity. From a young man who helped shape the landscape of our country, to an experienced world traveler with a full loving family - we hope this story brings you closer to the heritage of our country and inspires your families to document and share your stories too. Together we can reshape Canadian history to represent the multicultural roots that has created the Canada we know today.

From our family to yours, we hope you enjoy this great Canadian story.

- Kimberly Louise Elliott, Curly's loving granddaughter.

Content

My Formative Years:
Farm Life in The Great Depression

It was a bright and sunny Sunday morning when I came into this world, September 9th, 1928. My birth was of no great significance, but the location was historic. I was born in the Red Cross Outpost hospital at Paddockwood, Saskatchewan. This was the first such outpost hospital in the British Empire. I was the fourth boy and the middle child of a family of seven.

The Red Cross Outpost hospital, Paddockwood, Saskatchewan

The seven siblings of the Elliott family are as follows:

Orlin Keay	Sept. 23rd, 1921
Charles Wilfred	May 8th, 1923
Marshal Bruce	Nov. 11th, 1926
Allan Glen	Sept. 9th, 1928
Margaret Lucretia	April 27th, 1932
Stewart Norman	Aug. 6th, 1936
Morris Burton	Nov. 27th, 1939

To say that I grew up in the bush would be no exaggeration. Paddockwood was at the very north end of the agricultural area (at that time) and we were towards the northern edge of the farming district. This area is north of Prince Albert and was late in being surveyed. It was covered with a thick growth of poplar trees with a few patches of spruce interspersed. The soil was very rich, but it took a lot of hard work to clear and make it into farmland. The first homesteaders began arriving in the area in early 1911. By the end of that year 13 homesteaders had settled in the area and filed on their quarter sections of land. The area still did not have a name. A Post-Office was officially opened in 1913 in the home of the first mail carrier, Fred Pitts, a native of Paddockwood, Kent, UK. He apparently picked the name for Paddockwood. My Grandpa Charles Keay spent three years farming in the Chamberlain area of Saskatchewan before deciding to move north to take advantage of the better farmland.

Grandpa Charles arrived in Paddockwood on December 2, 1914 and immediately started cutting poplar trees where he wanted to build his house. A house and barn were completed, and the family moved in on Christmas Eve. The poplar logs were still frozen and when they began to warm up both the house and barn started sprouting new leaves. As the result of a newspaper ad Dad scouted the area and filed on his homestead on October 9, 1915. Our families and Grandpa Keay were about four miles apart.

All, or most of the above information, can be found in the 1911 - 1982 Paddockwood history book entitled Cordwood and Courage.[1] I have two copies of this book and you should take good care of them as they not only show my early family history but also paint a picture of rural life at that time. The second book you want to keep is the one prepared by our family in 1990 after Mum and Dad's passing. It was done in their memory and is entitled Looking Ahead by Preserving the Past.[2] I bought four of these books for our family so each of you should have one. Unfortunately, I cannot put my hands on mine at the present but lucky for me I have a copy of it through my cousin Duncan Robertson. Duncan is the son of Dad's youngest sister Florence. He was director of the Kelsey Institute of Applied Arts and Sciences in Saskatoon. He did a great amount of genealogy research on both the Elliott and Robertson families. Both Duncan and his wife Lorraine have passed away. Duncan died on January 11th, 2014 when I was on my South American adventure. He was cremated and I was fortunate enough to be at the internment

1.Cordwood and Courage: 1911-1982: Paddockwood, Beaton, Chesley, Chiefswood, Dorothy I-II, Elkholme, Elkrange, Birchbark, Howard Creek, Melba, Moose Lake, Pine Valley, Surrey. Paddockwood & District History Book, 1982.
2. Elliott Family History book

of his ashes at the Bradwell Cemetery on June 21st, 2014. Bradwell is just south east of Saskatoon where Grandpa Elliott first homesteaded when he moved west from Wawanesa Manitoba. Dad spent some of his youth there before moving into Saskatoon. Grandpa Elliott and the Robertson families were some of the first settlers in Bradwell and are buried side by side in the cemetery. Duncan gave most of his notes, maps, letters, etc. to me and the Elliott family history is contained in a brown hard covered three ring binder.

Enough about books and the past now onto my story. In 1929, one year after I was born, the world economy totally collapsed in what became known as the great depression. This lasted until the beginning of the Second World War in 1939 or through the first 12 years of my life. This had a very serious effect on people living in cities and towns but was not nearly so disastrous for the rural population. If you don't have anything to start with it's hard to lose it.

At that time most of the farms were small and the families large. Almost everyone was farming with horses and there were very few tractors in the area. I don't remember but apparently Dad did have a tractor at one time but either gave it back or lost it for inability to make payments. The only tractor I remember was an old 4 hp Fordson on steel wheels. This was not powerful enough for breaking new land and too slow for most farming tasks. We used it mostly for belt work and I shovelled many bushels of grain into a grinder powered by that noisy old monster. During the war Dad and I also used it to grade the dirt roads in our area. I drove the tractor and Dad ran the grader. I don't think we got any money for this, but it was a way of paying taxes. Dad also did some commercial grain grinding for the neighbours.

One good thing about having a tractor during the war was that as farmers we could buy purple gas. Regular gasoline was rationed and doled out on coupons. Purple gas set out in the sun for a few days in clear glass bottles lost its colour and "voila" Dad had gas for his Model "T" Ford truck.

I don't remember too much of my early childhood, but I apparently started my lifelong adventuring journey at a very young age, and I have the scar to prove it. Before the days of natural gas or electricity all homes in the bush country were heated by firewood. This meant that the logs had to be cut into short blocks before they could be used. This was all done by hand with a Swede saw. The saw was always left on the sawhorse with the blade horizontal about a foot and a half off the ground. Apparently, I was running around waving my arms and having a good time as little boys do, when going by the saw I ran my right arm across the saw blade and cut it from the wrist to the elbow. No doubt this mishap soon came to my mother's attention, and probably the neighbours also heard me. It was four miles to the Red Cross hospital, so Mum simply patched me up herself. She used the homesteaders' tried-and-true method of holding the cut together with the membrane from a hen's egg and wrapping it tightly with a bandage. It must have worked because I'm still here and the scar is still visible. This scar became a prominent identification mark on my personnel file when I first joined the RCMP. I remember asking why it was so important for my identification and the answer was, "We may need it to identify your corpse someday." Lesson one - don't ask questions if you might not like the answer.

One of the earliest memories I have is of Mum coming home from the hospital with a new baby. I presume this would have been Margaret which would make me about four at the time. Another thing that stands out in my memory is being at a school picnic with Dad. There was a round wash tub filled with pop bottles being cooled in icy water. The bottles were smaller than the current beer bottle and I remember Dad bought me one all for myself. I thought he was just about the richest guy in the world and I was a really lucky kid.

All my formal education was in a one room school as even the Paddockwood High School had only one room. Our district and school was called Chesley. It was given that name by Dad who named it after his school of the same name at Wawanesa, Manitoba. That school was named by Grandpa Orlin S. Elliott, who likely named it after the Chesley area in Ontario from where many of the Elliotts migrated. Chesley School was a mile and a quarter east and a half a mile north of our place which meant it was about a two-mile walk to school.

The school was a typical one room building with a bank of windows on the east side as there were no lights or electricity. There was a horse barn for about eight horses plus the two outdoor toilets and a well for water. There was a wood furnace in the basement but since the school did not have a teacherage (a small cottage on site where the teacher lived) there was no one to attend the furnace overnight. Either the teacher or some older student living nearby had the job of lighting the furnace and getting the school warmed up in the morning.

Chesley School like most others of that era was the social centre of the community. It was not only used for learning activities but for meetings, dances, card parties, church services and social gatherings. During a couple of weeks in summer it was also headquarters for the Anglican Church Van ladies, otherwise known as Sunday School by Post. Dad was very strict about us boys playing around on the school grounds if any religious activities were going on in the school.

Photo taken around the time I started school in 1934
Allan   Orlin   Grandpa Elliott Bruce Charlie
Margaret

I don't remember how I got to school when I was really young. I expect for the most part I walked carrying my Rogers Syrup lunch pail like everyone else. We didn't have a light carriage or Bennett buggy and the only other way during the summer would be on horseback. I remember my older brothers riding horses, but I don't remember riding double or on my own. In the wintertime we had a one-horse toboggan which Charlie usually drove. In the summer we had our secret shortcuts through the bush. This allowed us to work on our slingshot accuracy and play "Cowboys and Indians" along the way. If it was not too cold or wet during the summer, we also got to go to school in our bare feet. Runners were unheard of at that time and we all wore boots, usually handed down from an older brother.

The School Superintendent came once a year to inspect the school and rate the teacher. Everyone was expected to be on their best behaviour during his visit. He usually had a bigger and newer car than anyone else and this was a big attraction for us boys. I don't know of any farmer who bought a new car during the depression. Another visitor to the school during the year was the traveling dental clinic. This was not looked forward to with any great anticipation because it usually meant that any bad teeth were pulled. There was no such thing as filling them at that time, nor was parental authorization necessary. With thirty or so students to go through in a few hours, freezing was quick and extraction even quicker.

Two of the biggest events during the year were the summer picnic at the end of the school term and the Christmas concert. The picnics consisted of sporting events like foot races, high jump, long jumps and ball games. There was also homemade ice cream and goodies at the end of the day. The Christmas concert was a huge event for the whole family. Every student in school usually had some part in the concert while their parents sat, watching, on planks propped up on blocks of wood. Santa Claus always arrived to the ringing of bells and brought small gifts of candy or nuts for the younger students. The older students knew all about Santa Claus and were lucky to get a new scribbler or some other needed school supply.

I don't remember if there was a dance after the Christmas concert or not, but dances were one of the favourite social events in the area. Word went around by word of mouth that a dance was being held and there was always good attendance. The whole family came to these dances, grandmas and grandpas, parents and kids. When the kids got tired, they usually went to sleep on coats or blankets piled on top the desks, which were pushed over to the side of the room. The Chesley orchestra was comprised of my brother Orlin, Ernie Smith and Sid Stewart. Dad would call the square dances and sometimes chip in with his bones. If you are not familiar with these musical items, they are eight-inch pieces of hardwood in the shape of rib bones. Dad could hold four in each hand and by flicking his wrist could rattle them like a drum and keep the beat for any kind of music. I inherited four of these bones and my brother Bruce got the other half. I cannot even hold two in one hand, nor can I make them rattle.

There is an extensive write up on Chesley School # 4302 in the C. & C. book.[3] My brother Charlie has an interesting article in this book on his time and recollections of the Chesley School. All of the teachers are listed but the only one I really remember is Mrs. Aschim. She was there for a number of years and boarded with the Everett and Mary Jones family who were some of our best friends. The first teacher at Chesley School was a Miss Olive Freeman. She boarded with Mum and Dad in 1921 when Orlin was a baby. She went on to marry John Diefenbaker and became wife of the 13th Prime Minister of Canada. To us she was always "Aunty

3. Cordwood and Courage: 1911-1982: Paddockwood, Beaton, Chesley, Chiefswood, Dorothy I-II, Elkholme, Elkrange, Birchbark, Howard Creek, Melba, Moose Lake, Pine Valley, Surrey. Paddockwood & District History Book, 1982.

Olive" and was a frequent Paddockwood is in the federal riding of Prince Albert which was represented by John Diefenbaker. He was not the only prime minister to have P.A. as their federal riding because it was also held by the Liberal Prime Minister, William Lyon Mackenzie King. King came to Paddockwood once every four years when there was a federal election. I remember one time, likely during the war years, when it was announced that he would be speaking at the Paddockwood Village Hall. This was a big deal to a lot of the kids who looked forward to meeting the Prime Minister, saying hello, shaking his hands and doing all that neat stuff. Dad was not a liberal and there was no way the Elliott kids were going to go to town just to speak to that damn "Liberal buffoon." So, I did not get to see, speak to or shake hands with the 10th and longest serving prime minister in Canadian history. However, I am not and have never been a Liberal, either by inclination, philosophy or ballot, so I guess I didn't miss too much.

There was one event which was okay with Dad and that was the visitation of the King and Queen to Canada in 1939. On their train trip across the country they made a stop in Saskatoon. I don't know how it was arranged but most of the kids from Chesley School got to go and see their Majesties. I was probably one of the youngest ones as I would be only ten at the time. We went in the back of a farm truck that had a solid grain box on the bottom but only a cattle rack on top.[4] This provided very little protection from the wind. There were hard plank benches to sit on but that's about all. We packed our lunches and left very early in the morning as it was at least a four-hour drive to Saskatoon.

I remember that when we got to Saskatoon, we were met by some Boy Scouts. They led us to the parade route and got us set up for when the Queen and King came by in their open car. We saw them for about a minute. We waved our hands, some with flags and we could clap but we were not supposed to shout. The scouts then had us run two blocks through the city to another street and we got to see them for the second time on their way back to the train station. It was a full and exciting day and I can still remember it quite vividly. Apparently, it was a bit much for me as I'm told I was sound asleep in the bottom of the truck when we got home.

With a one room school and as many as 40 students the teacher had to be an organizational genius. As I remember we usually started with an organizational genius. As I remember we usually started with an assembly and sang one of the national anthems either, God Save the King or O Canada. Singing was an accepted part of the day's activities and everyone sang - maybe not too good but we all sang. Some mornings the teacher also conducted a health inspection where she checked your hands and fingernails to see if they were clean. And oh yes, you had to have a clean handkerchief. This gave rise to the boys all having a "shower and a blower", one to use and one for inspections. After the opening formalities the teacher would start each grade and age group working on their own particular subject. She would then give more specific instructions to the various classes as needed or as their turn came up. This meant that everyone in school could listen to the teacher no matter what class she was teaching. Each student could get individual help as needed by holding up your hand. You learned to concentrate on your own work and surprisingly the system worked. Any misbehaving and you would stay in over recess, after school or clean the blackboard and brushes and in serious cases you held out your hand and got the strap. Not a good idea as your parents invariably found out that you had been strapped, which meant you had likely been really bad and you usually got another one at home. The teacher was always held in very high esteem by the parents and could do no wrong. Some teachers were also inclined to wrap you over the knuckles with a long ruler for misbehaving and that hurt even more than the strap. Of course, I never had any of those things happen to me!!!!!

My three years of high school were pretty much a bust. In 1939 Paddockwood School was expanded due to increasing membership. By 1941 it was overcrowded again, and the school board rented the Friendship Hall for the high school classes. This like the Chesley School was a one room building. It was heated with a woodstove and there were no inside facilities. It did however have electric lights. To call it a high school was a real stretch of the imagination. It was more like a meeting place to take a correspondence course. It was also difficult to retain teachers as it was not a high-end position. The teachers were always looking for better opportunities which frequently meant joining the armed services. I walked to school one morning only to find a note on the door stating, "Teacher has joined up."

Orlin joined the Royal Canadian Air Force in 1941 and Charlie followed him in 1943. Dad was busy selling Rawleigh[5] products trying to raise some cash, and that left Mum, Bruce and I to run the farm. We were still farming with horses and only had a section of land at that time. Bruce and I missed a lot of school days, especially Bruce. I usually rode my bike to school when weather permitted and during the winter, I walked the 3 1/2 miles each way morning and night. You can

5. Cordwood and Courage: 1911-1982: Paddockwood, Beaton, Chesley, Chiefswood, Dorothy I-II, Elkholme, Elkrange, Birchbark, Howard Creek, Melba, Moose Lake, Pine Valley, Surrey, Paddockwood & District History Book, 1982, p. 195.

understand my disappointment upon arriving at school and finding there was no teacher.

When Orlin was discharged from the Air Force in 1946 he and Shirley rented a small house in town. That winter I stayed with them some nights, rather than walking home.

Elliott siblings 1942
Allan Bruce Charlie Orlin Stewart
Margaret Morris

Because of the teacher fiascos at the Paddockwood High School we were never taught such compulsory subjects as algebra, trigonometry or any of the required official second languages, German, French or Latin. As a result of this no certificate stating that you had successfully completed a grade was ever issued and you just moved on each year to the next grade. The results being that when push comes to shove, I can only produce a grade eight certificate. Not too bad for a rural country boy at that time, but throughout all my life I wished I had completed High School. I did get to university when I took a bunch of evening adult courses at the University of Calgary while working for the Royal Bank. I enjoyed the university experience and did very well as I loved doing the reading and research, and for a few extra bucks my secretaries would type up my papers.

There are a few adventures I should mention before going on to my policing career. The first one which my sister Margaret and everyone else seems to remember is my little trip down the well - headfirst. Every farm in the Paddockwood area had a hand dug well and we were no exception. Ours was conveniently located in the middle of the farmyard, was 2' x 4' square 30 feet deep and lined with boards. With no electricity the well was also the refrigerator and a place to hang your cream between shipments to the creamery in Prince Albert. Ours was like all others and had a rope and pulley, the pulley being suspended on a bracket seven or eight feet above the well.

By the end of the summer the water in our well was fairly low and you were lucky if there were 2 or 3 feet of water. To fill the water bucket, you had to give the rope a flick to turn the bucket sideways otherwise it would just sit on the bottom. With the low water you might say I was at the end of my rope and was holding on with one hand up near the pulley while looking down to see where the bucket was sitting. I was leaning on the rope as it slipped through my upper hand and I was heading downstream headfirst. I obviously hit the cream can with the back of my neck and soon found myself sitting in very cold muddy water. At that point the fun was all over, but the real excitement and my extraction from the bowels of the earth was just beginning.

I was down a well with the only rope long enough and strong enough to pull me out. It wasn't very long before a very anxious mother, soon followed by several other faces appeared in the opening above me. They were all screaming at once as to my welfare and what the hell I was doing down the well. The first thing we had to do was retrieve the rope. This was accomplished by tying several halter shanks together and dropping them down to me. They didn't trust me enough to tie myself to the rope so hauled it up, prepared a loop for me and dropped it down again. I secured myself and was duly recovered by Bruce and Charlie. They were considerate enough to have removed the can of cream first so that I didn't hit it again on the way up. I think the water was forgotten for that night but was declared drinkable by the next morning.

I was certainly bruised and battered after this little adventure but did not appear to be seriously injured. My neck was particularly sore and after a couple of days Dad took me to see the doctor in Prince Albert. I don't recall having any x-rays and received no medication or physiotherapy. However, I did not come out of this unscathed as I still have a lump on one of the vertebra in my neck from hitting the cream can. I contribute this to some extent for my stooped posture and it still reminds me once in a while that falling down wells is not for the faint of heart.

Margaret drawing water from the well

Grandpa Charles Keay, Mum's Dad, was always one of our favourite relatives and visitors. There were four children in the Keay family. Mum, Euphemia "Effie" was the oldest followed by Charles "Chick", James "Jim" and the youngest Margaret, whom we always knew as Aunt May. Grandma Keay died in 1929 when I was just a year old. Grandpa Keay originally lived in the Melba school district which was about four miles south of where we lived. He farmed with his brother Bill and Aunt Kate when they first came to Canada from Scotland. Grandpa was very active in the organization of the schools and community affairs. He was also active in the building of the first Paddockwood community hall and was likewise involved in dances and socials. According to Mum, Uncle Bill was quite musical and played the violin at dances throughout the Paddockwood area. About the only thing I remember of Aunt Kate on the farm was that she was a rather large woman who gave us boys raisins to eat. This was a real treat for us, and we made them last as long as possible by only eating one at a time. Bill and Aunt Kate were not cut out to be farmers and moved to the United States sometime before the start of the Second World War. They had no children and Bill died when he was fairly young. Kate remarried and lived in Seattle, Washington. I visited with her once when I was in the Force and holidaying in Victoria with Uncle Chick.

Grandpa and Grandma Keay left Paddockwood in about 1927 and turned their farm over to Uncle Jim and Aunt Jean. They had two adopted children, David and Sheila. Grandpa took on the position of janitor/cleaner at King George School in Prince Albert. He and Grandma lived on the top floor of the school, which was really part of the attic made into living quarters. Aunt May married Bram Vanderkracht shortly before the war started. When Bram joined the Army and was sent overseas, she moved in with Grandpa and that is where I have many fond memories of her. King George was an eight-room school on a hill on the south side of Prince Albert and was one of the highest points in the city. From their kitchen window you could see all of the downtown area. Bruce and I got to spend Christmas with Grandpa when we were fourteen and supposedly old enough to behave ourselves. I remember how excited I was when it finally became my turn. Of course, I liked being with Grandpa and was never far from his side.

I remember distinctly that the school was heated by a monstrous wood furnace in the basement. This furnace took four-foot lengths of cordwood which Grandpa chucked into the basement through a wood chute. There were rows and rows of cordwood stacked up by the school and Grandpa had a hand sleigh which we would load up and haul over to the basement chute. We would then throw the wood through the chute into the basement - snow and all. It took several loads to keep the furnace going just for the night. There were also many pails of ashes to be hauled out plus all the rooms and halls had to be swept every day. There were no elevators and with four flights of stairs from top to bottom grandpa was certainly in good shape. By the end of the day I was happy to help Aunt May with some of the kitchen duties.

Grandpa would always drive out to our farm three or four times during the summer. He had the most fascinating old car which I remember as a Reo Flying Cloud coupe with a rumble seat. One summer he took Bruce and I with a couple of our friends on a camping trip to Christopher Lake. I remember tying all our camping and cooking gear onto the fenders and some in the backseat. With four of us, two got to ride inside and two rode in the rumble seat. I even remember that Grandpa made us change off so that we all got a turn at riding in the outside back seat. Seat belts were unheard of and we could horse around and do anything we wanted to as long as we didn't fall out. He had a friend at Bell's Beach, where we got to set up our tent. We also had the use of a rowboat and Grandpa took us fishing both morning and night. He did all the rowing and Lord help you if you were dragging that green line and spoon with the tiniest bit of grass attached. He would let you know in no uncertain terms that we were after fish not salad. We did catch lots of jackfish and had fish fries twice a day. There was no such thing as sleeping bags, so we had a tent, a tarp and a blanket each for us kids. It was an exciting, wonderful three days provided and supervised by a kindly loving grandpa. I don't remember the names of the two friends that went with us, but I do remember what a great time it was and even swimming in the lake "sans bathing suit." Christopher Lake was a pretty remote and undeveloped paradise at that time.

When you were a kid growing up in the depression a trip anywhere of more than 10 miles was something to get excited about. This was especially so if it was a trip to a lake. I remember when our entire school went on two such excursions. The first was to Christopher Lake and the second one was to Waskesiu in Prince Albert National Park. These school excursions were by a farm truck similar to our visit to the King and Queen in Saskatoon. All such trips unfortunately stopped when the war started as gasoline was rationed.

When I was about 16, Buddy Roach, Glen Jeffries and I talked our parents into letting us ride our bikes to Candle Lake for a little holiday. Buddy's dad, Pete Roach, had just made a homemade boat and we were anxious to try it out. It was a pretty crude affair, not much more than three boards wide on the bottom, two high on the sides and pointed at the front end. The oars were made with thin wooden rails with a flat board for the blade. To let us go off on our own was really exciting and we spent days discussing plans for our big adventure. Sleeping bags were still unheard of then so just like my camping trip with Grandpa, all we would have is a tarp, probably a blanket each, one pot, a frying pan, our own tin plates and a fork. A spoon was not necessary, and we all had our trusty jackknifes. We did have a small axe for chopping wood and a good supply of matches. Our fishing gear would have been no more than some green fishing line wrapped around the board and a couple of Len Thompson spoons.

We had carriers on our bikes, both front and back and with them loaded down we still made the 25-mile ride to Candle Lake in record time. There was only one commercial enterprise on the lake at that time and it was not much more than a store, service station and a short wooden dock. We checked in with the owner, stowed our bikes, loaded up the boat with our supplies and took off. We had never thought of telling anyone where we were headed as that was going to be our secret hideaway. Our plans were to go to an island on the far side of the lake which looked a lot closer than it turned out to be when we started rowing. When we got out into the open water the waves became a little bigger and Glen immediately got sick and nearly fell overboard when he was throwing up. We made him sit in the bottom of the boat for the rest of the trip.

We eventually reached the island, built a lean-to, threw our tarp over it, made a fire pit and everything was ready for two days of pure kids' fun. We were Huckleberry Finns without a care in the world. We caught fish right from the shore and ate them every way we could think about, fried, boiled, burnt on a stick or baked in mud in the fire. If they didn't turn out, you threw them back and in two minutes could catch another one. We played in the water until we were tired, played knife games, chased each other around the island like Indians and didn't have a care in the world. On the last morning we caught fish to take home and made the long row back across the lake. On arrival at the dock the owner had some fatherly advice for us and how dumb, stupid and totally irresponsible we had been not to tell someone of our plans and where we were staying. They were about ready to send a search party looking for us.

Our adventures were not quite over yet as on the way home the weight on my front carrier caused the hub on the wheel to break and the little ball bearings went

13

flying off into space. My bike became unrideable. After a little trial and error, we found a way to fill the space between the hub and axle with green willows cut to the full width of the hub. This held the wheel straight enough that I was able to push my bike if I held it slightly to one side. And that is exactly what I did for the last 10 or 12 miles coming home. Buddy and Glen had to take all our fish. Needless to say, Mum was happy to see me even if I was late and the fish were not in the "freshest" of condition by that time.

Bicycle parts were hard to come by in the rural areas but somewhere Dad found a bent front wheel with a usable hub and Ernie Smith, the local blacksmith, re-spoked the wheel for me. Within a week I was back in the saddle again, none the worse after my trip, but a whole lot smarter. The wonderful memories of that first summer holiday away from home some seventy years ago are still fresh in my mind.

The summer after our fishing trip the three of us, myself, Bud and Glen decided we needed something more exciting and planned a "bear hunting expedition." Glen's family lived north of Chesley School right on the edge of the forested area. There was a trail leading from their place into the hunting area and a trapper's cabin that we could use. Bud provided the team of horses, the wagon and also the bear-trap which we were going to use to catch the ferocious beasties.

The Sunday before our adventure the three of us were fixing a bridge over a deep creek in order that we could cross it with the team and wagon. Bud as usual had his 30-30 with him and I had my trusty single shot 22. All afternoon, being kids, someone was forever shouting "there's a bear - there's a bear." Sure enough, in mid-afternoon a two-year-old black bear came walking down the road right towards us. Someone spotted him and raised the alarm and of course the one nearest our guns didn't pay any attention and Mr. Bear walked off into the woods. It did however confirm our hopes that the woods were crawling with bears and we would each come home with at least one. That was not to be the case and he was the only bear we saw.

The trip to the cabin was uneventful and it was camping in luxury compared to the year before. We set up our bear trap baited with a gallon jar of rotten home canned fish. We could smell it a mile away, but the bears were apparently not interested in it. The first night at the cabin we heard a timber wolf howling/calling and after a day of searching we located the wolf den. We saw the bitch run off, but she didn't go too far and kept watching us from the edge of the bush. We took a couple of shots at her but without success. Now we had a problem. The mother wolf was watching us, we didn't know how many more of the pack were around and we had a den full of pups that we had to secure. The den was on the south side of a sandy knoll with lots of downed trees and trash around. We had a shovel and an axe back at the cabin, but we didn't want to leave one alone with just a single shot 22, not knowing how many wolves were in the area. In the end we decided to plug up all the den entrances we could find with sticks and cover them with logs so the bitch could not dig them out before we could all run to the cabin and back.

Our plan worked and we were able to dig down into the den where the pups were hiding. They were about the size of a small coyote and put up a snarling good defence. One got away but we got all the rest. I can't remember for sure, but I think that we also got the bitch as she kept making closer and closer feints to protect her litter. We brought home four carcasses, the game warden confirmed that they were Timberwolves and paid us a reward. I don't know just how much it was, but it seemed like a lot of money at that time. As Timberwolves had killed off almost our entire flock of sheep and were taking calves in the area, no one was unhappy that we had killed the mother and her cubs. In fact, we were heroes for a while - well at least a day.

The foregoing saga was not our first contact with Timberwolves. In the winter of 1940, a pack of Timberwolves came through our yard one night and killed 28 sheep out of a flock of about 30, some had just been bought that day. We heard no barking by the dog or noise from the sheep. It was a terrible surprise in the morning to find dead or dying sheep all over the yard. That morning was the closest I ever came to seeing my Dad cry. It also finished the idea of raising sheep. My brother Orlin and a neighbour tracked the wolves for a day and a half and eventually managed to kill one. There was no love for wolves in any northern farming community.

Growing up on a farm in the Dirty Thirties was not always fun, games and adventure. I remember there were still a lot of poplar bush trees on our farm and they had to be removed to make forest into farmland. Dad, Orlin and Charlie would grub around the roots of the tree and then pull it over with a team of horses. The stump would be cut off to be burnt and the tree saved for firewood. Bruce and I would carry the branches and other small bits and pieces to be piled on the stumps for burning. I would have been no more than ten or eleven years old at that time. The brush piles were left for at least a year before being burnt. The land then had to be turned over with a breaking plow, sometimes pulled by six horses or if you were lucky, a rented tractor. This was followed by a heavy one-way disc, then a root harrow and after that there were more roots to be picked, piled and burnt. There was always lots of work for every age, strength and ability. Our 160-acre quarter section was not fully cleared until after Charlie returned from the Royal Canadian Air Force in 1946.

When Orlin joined the Air Force in early 1941, followed by Charlie in 1943, and with Dad away all week selling Rawleigh products, the running of the farm was basically left up to Bruce and me. We were still farming with horses, as was most everyone else. The horses, cows and all the barn stuff were basically left to Bruce, while I looked after Mum and the household chores. That meant looking after the pigs, chickens, household waste, firewood, water and all other endless items needed around a farmhouse. In the summer we also had a huge garden which was Mum's and my responsibility. I spent much more time with Mum than any of the other boys and I'm sure she considered me her favourite. Any social graces or common sense I may have I attribute to her and she was the best friend I've ever had.

Another thing Mum and I did was pick raspberries together. There were no raspberries on our farm, but the Joneses who lived two miles east of us had great wild raspberry patches. The picking season was short so when the berries were ripe Mum and I would walk to the Joneses in the morning with our two 10-pound Rogers syrup pails. We would pick one pail each in the morning. We would then have dinner (in the traditional sense of the word, which to this day is how I refer to "lunch") and the ladies would clean what we picked in the morning. We would proceed to pick another pail each and carry the four full pails home. I remember them getting awfully heavy by the time we got home and those wire handles sure cut into your hands. Mum would have them all canned in quart sealers before she went to bed that night and then we would do the same thing the next day. The raspberry picking would last for a week or longer.

The Elliott family had another long-standing tradition with the Everett and Mary Jones family. We shared every Christmas and New Year's together. One-year Christmas would be at our house and New Year's at the Joneses and the following year the locations would be reversed. This had been going on since 1929 and was still a tradition when I left in 1947. Not only were the two families together but every old bachelor in the country seemed to have an automatic invitation and always knew which house to go to for the festive dinner. How our mothers ever managed to cook a turkey dinner and all the trimmings for 15 or 20 people I'll never know.

At the start of World War II in 1939 the population of the village of Paddockwood would probably be less than 200. The C. & C.1 history book lists the names of 239 men and women who joined the Armed Services from the Paddockwood area. This meant that there was a severe shortage of able-bodied men during the harvest season. I got my first paying job stooking for Pat O'Hea when I was 15 years old. I worked for him after I got my own chores done. Buddy Roach helped me and together we stooked the better part of a quarter section. Pat O'Hea was a fine old Irish gentleman bachelor but he would not put up with shoddy work and we had to go back and reset many of our stooks that had fallen over. That fall I also handled a team of horses and hay rack when they were threshing on our farm. I would never have made it without the help of a couple of those same old bachelors who came for Christmas.

Getting back to Pat O'Hea, he was one of the first homesteaders in the area and picked the site for the village of Paddockwood. He farmed with horses all his life and ploughed his little garden plot with a single horse. This was obviously an old Indian camping ground and he frequently turned up arrowheads. He seemed to have been fond of me and eventually gave me a box of arrowheads which I have subsequently turned over to Lee, my third and youngest son and avid historian. Pat O'Hea is written up on page 396 of the C. & C. history book.[6]

When I was 16, I put in a couple of days away from home on the Ole Erickson threshing crew. It was a long day from 4.00 in the morning till 9.00 at night but I survived. By the next fall I was a full-fledged member of the threshing crew and had my own team and wagon for the entire threshing circuit. There is a picture of the Erickson threshing outfit on page 623 of the C. & C. book. In that photo, I don't know if that's me waving or not, but I was certainly there. The threshing machine was a 36-inch model, the biggest made, and you fed sheaves into it from both sides at the same time. It took eight bundle teams going steady to keep up a constant supply of sheaves. Now all this and much more is done by one man with a combine.

After 70 years it is difficult for me to remember too much about the routine of my teenage years. I do know that we had several summer visitations from aunts and cousins, but the details are rather vague. I also remember that these visitations usually corresponded with the height of the gardening season when the peas, beans and carrots were at their best. One time Mum and I picked a whole wash tub

6. Cordwood and Courage: 1911-1982: Paddockwood, Beaton, Chesley, Chiefswood, Dorothy I-II, Elkholme, Elkrange, Birchbark, Howard Creek, Melba, Moose Lake, Pine Valley, Surrey, Paddockwood & District History Book, 1982.

full of peas and the next day these two aunts showed up with their daughters in tow. Mum and the two aunts spent the afternoon shelling peas. A bag of peas together with one of beans and another of carrots went home with them. All my hard work in the garden was offset by the joy of having two young girls in the house. They were about the same age as Bruce and I and we did have fun together. We played all sorts of tricks on them like having them ride the calves or try milking cows. The girls entertained us by tap dancing and that was a real novelty. Although I don't remember names the aunts would be descendants from Dad's sister Mable who married into the McCallum clan.

Dad and I at about the same age

As I look back over all those years, I'm still amazed and in awe at how Mum could handle adversity and stressful situations with such grace and calm. When unexpected guests arrived, she would simply say, "Allan it's time to kill that old rooster", or one of the old hens that was not laying eggs anymore - and that was my cue to go and do just that. I would catch a chicken, chop the head off, pull the big feathers out and by that time Mum would have a kettle of hot water boiling. We had our own system for pouring boiling hot water over the chicken to loosen the feathers and in a half-hour, we had a bird ready for the oven. If the garden was ready, I would gather some fresh vegetables and that's all Mum needed for a delicious dinner. Sometimes she would bake a pie and if not, there was always her canned raspberries and a slice of freshly made bread. All this was done without electricity or running water while looking after three younger children plus the guests. Margaret is four years younger than me and I was definitely Mum's chore boy when it came to helping around the house. I didn't realize there was such a significant bond between us until much later in life and of course by then it was too late to tell her. Another regret covered by my favourite saying "Too soon old - too late smart."

Looking back on life I feel I was fortunate, not unlucky to have been a farm kid during the Great Depression. Yes, we were dirt poor and had no running water, electricity or telephone - nor did anyone else. We wore hand-me-down clothes and shirts made from checkered flour sacks, but so did everyone else. We had a school with good teachers and received a basic education above that of most of our parents. We were free to run and play at will, crime was unheard of, we had neighbours who looked after each other and we were a community.

Although we were certainly poor, I was never once hungry or starving for food. The food may have been boring, not the most nutritious or best, but never once

Me leaving home - Dad's model T Ford

was I hungry. The farm families were much better off than the city people. We not only had our own supply of meat, milk, chickens, eggs, butter etc. but our large gardens supplied enough vegetables for the whole year. Add to this the preserving of both tame and wild fruits provided some additional variety to our daily diet.

Looking back there are many, many times when I wish that I had done more to further my education. However, by the time I was eighteen I wanted to get away, see the world and have some fun. I knew that farming and shovelling manure for the rest of my life was not for me. I was also in a no-win situation with my schooling. I supposedly had three years of High School - when in reality I had learned nothing useful. I could not have gone on into Grade XII, nor could I have picked up all the missing subjects without starting all over again. The only career that I ever wanted was to be a "Mountie" and that was the path I chose. The road ahead was clear - but it was not an easy one.

The Mountie Years

During the Second World War a great number of the RCMP members were released for military service. They went overseas as the No. 1 Provost Corps. Others did not reengage after their five-year term was up so that they could join the armed services. There would also have been a number of retirements. With the return to peacetime activities and all the soldiers returning to civilian activities, there was a great need for a rapid increase in the overall strength of the RCMP. To accomplish this the age of engagement was reduced to 18 years. Across the prairies hundreds of kids like myself seized upon this opportunity to get away from the drudgery of farming, have some excitement and wear that famous scarlet coat.

On November 6th, 1946, I approached the Prince Albert RCMP Detachment with a view of joining up. They were not very encouraging and told me that my chances were about 1 in 75 applications. However, if I wanted to proceed, they would set up an appointment for me to write the entrance exam. I wrote my exam a couple of weeks later and I flunked math. I was thoroughly disappointed but not too surprised. With some of the math questions I had no idea whatsoever what they were talking about. In grade school we were taught *arithmetic* not *mathematics*. We could do our 12 times tables forward or backwards, add, subtract, divide, plus fractions etc., but subjects like algebra, geometry or trigonometry were neither in our curriculum or vocabulary. Fortunately, I think the kindly old Sergeant recognized both my disappointment and determination. He assured me that if I went home and studied up on my math, I could have another rewrite on just the math portion. I would have to wait three months before I could try again. This I did and the second time around, on May 28th, 1947, I was successful. I don't know whether I passed with flying colours or just squeaked through, but it didn't matter, I was in - I was on my way. Little did I know what lay ahead.

About a month later I received the welcome letter that I was accepted and was to report to a doctor in Prince Albert for my medical examination. My medical was on May 20th, all was going well, and I remember the doctor with a big grin on his face as he told me I had a flat foot, which was alright as policemen were called "Flatfoot." Then he dropped the bombshell "But, you have a hernia and I can't pass you." I'm sure with tears in my eyes I asked, "What's a hernia?" He assured me that it could be fixed with surgery and after recovery I would have a clear medical. My Mum was disappointed, but Dad took it in stride and started arranging for my operation. How they paid for it or what it cost, I have no idea, but there was no health care or insurance at that time. There was no such thing as arthroscopic surgery, and I laid flat on my back for seven days before I was even allowed to stand up. After recuperating for another couple of months I passed my final medical and on June 27th and was interviewed by a Senior Personnel Officer. I survived that and was approved to go. What a relief, joy and excitement all around. On August 8th, 1947 I received a letter that had been a long time coming. I was instructed to report to the Prince Albert RCMP detachment on August 29 where I would receive a train ticket to Regina. It was almost a full year since I had made my first inquiry into the possibility of becoming Mountie.

There was lots of excitement around home as I had to get some decent clothes. I ended up with a pair of slacks, a couple of shirts, a ball jacket and some underwear. Dad was thoughtful enough to put together a shaving kit for me as I was not shaving at the time. I had shaved a couple of times but I'm sure that was just because some of the other kids were trying to "out man" me. So, with 20 bucks in my pocket and a mother's love in my heart, I caught the bus for Prince Albert and set off on my great 26 year Royal Canadian Mounted Police adventure.

I don't think I slept too much the last night at home and I have no recollection of ever eating on the day I left. It was an overnight train ride to Regina and since I only had a seat ticket not a berth, I stayed up all night. I was met in Regina by a crabby old Corporal (Cpl.) named Fred Box. He dropped me off in front of the administration building and said, "You sign up in there" and drove away. I sat in a hallway for most of the morning. A few people did stop and talk to me, but it was close to noon by the time I was escorted before the Officer Commanding. After a few pertinent questions he gave me the Oath of Office for the Force and the Oath of Allegiance to the King. I was then turned over to a Sergeant and signed my life away for the next five years. As I was only 18, I was ranked as a Recruit Special Constable (RSC) #6994. It would be another year before I received my permanent Regimental #15338.

I had dinner in the mess hall which was a bit of an adventure but by mid-afternoon I was getting damn sleepy and was looking for a place to lie down. I don't remember how, but I guess somebody gave me instructions and I ended up on the third floor of "C" block. This was one of the oldest buildings in Depot and was rather a dilapidated barracks. Imagine my surprise when I reached the top of the stairs and found the whole floor was one big bedroom. Thirty-two beds, sixteen on each side, all in a perfectly straight line and immaculately made up. I walked up and down the room but could not find my name on any bed so picked one about halfway down the room, laid on top and went to sleep.

Before long I was awakened by some old bugger with a big moustache standing at the end of the room and screaming at me like a banshee on steroids. Beside him was a rather pompous looking officer with a great amount of scrambled eggs on the peak of his hat. I had no idea what he was trying to say or what I was supposed to do so figured my best course of action was to play dead and stay asleep. About 15 minutes later that old bugger with the moustache was back only this time he was the Sergeant Major (S/M). In very loud, rapid and colourful language he informed me that I gotten off to a very bad start by sleeping through the Commissioner's inspection. Commissioner (Commr.) - who the hell was he and who was he inspecting? I was the only one in the room and I was sleeping. Later on, I found out that the Commr. was Stuart Taylor Wood and it was a long-standing custom for the Superior Officer to inspect all the facilities as well as the men. Six years later I was stationed at Grande Prairie with his son Constable (Cst.) John Wood and we had a good laugh over my first meeting with his father. The most profound lesson I learned from that first day is that S/Ms are not normally nice people. They rank themselves only one rung below God himself and are to be avoided at all times and by whatever means possible.

Later that day I was assigned to another room with two other recruits, Harry Armstrong and Charles "Chuck" English. They had been in Regina mowing lawns for a week and were a big help with learning the ropes on military life and discipline.

Unknown, or unrealized by us was that we were being sent to Rockcliffe near Ottawa to fill out a squad already in training. Being a long weekend, nothing happened until Tuesday morning when we were informed that we were on our way to "N" Division in Rockcliffe, Ontario. We boarded the train that afternoon and arrived in Ottawa on Thursday. A week after joining the Force the consequences of my career decision were beginning to sink in. I was lonely, scared, a long way from home and I hadn't even had a chance to write my mother to tell her where to find me, nor had I reached my 19th birthday.

The morning after we arrived in Rockcliffe our first duty was to go to the QM stores and draw our kit. As we left the administration building there was an injured recruit lying on a stretcher on the sidewalk. He had apparently been kicked by a horse. When we came back an hour and a half later, he was still there as the ambulance had not yet arrived. We inquired of the Cpl. watching over him what the problem was, his answer was something to the effect "Oh, they are probably getting bids to see who can do it the cheapest." It was not an encouraging indicator of any future medical treatment but was a reminder not to get kicked by a horse.

The trip to the QM stores was mind boggling to say the least. I had never seen so much clothing for one person in my life and could not believe that it was all mine. You were issued with two of everything from underwear, socks, pants, shirts, jackets, ties, hats, boots, raingear and even a winter pea jacket. You got your own toothbrush, (stamped RCMP), polishing equipment for buttons and both black and brown polish for your shoes. You were also issued a riding crop, which was not for riding or as a billy stick, but for marching. You received a Sam Brown - but no pistol. That would come later. Everything issued was supposed to be your size, but some required a trip to the tailor shop for adjustments. After all that you still got your bedding, sheets, pillowcases, pillow and at least two blankets. One grey and one brown stamped RCMP which was to go on top of your bed. As well as your usual uniform we also got a set of fatigues which amounted to khaki pants and jacket. The fatigue jacket still came with brass buttons that had to be polished just like the rest. The fatigues were used for dirty work like mowing lawns and cleaning barns. When the issuing was completed, they gave you a large white canvas dunnage bag to hold everything. It was a struggle to get all our "stuff" back to barracks in one trip.

Harry Armstrong, Chuck English and I were the last to arrive and so got the last three of the 32 beds in the room. Naturally they were the farthest from the washrooms and exits stairs. You had no closets, only a shelf over your single bed and some hooks on the wall. Everything you owned was either to be on that shelf, hanging on the wall or stored neatly under your bed. Everything else had to be properly laid out on the bed every morning. With our first pay cheque almost everyone bought a trunk which would fit under your bed.

My first photo in uniform

We had the rest of the morning to get into uniform and sort out our gear. Right after lunch we joined Squad No.42, which had been in training all week. No allowances were made for the training we had missed, and we were thrown into a steep learning curve, especially when it came to marching or understanding certain orders. After getting shouted at a few times you soon learned to follow the herd. As Squad No. 42 was formed up in Rockcliffe well over half the members were from eastern Canada. There were a few from the prairies but I think I was the only one from Saskatchewan.

There were only two members out of the 32 recruits who were over 21 years old. I was likely the youngest and was most certainly the "greenest of the green." I had never associated with or interacted with such a large number of similar aged young men. I was rather timid and not used to pushing and fighting for my place in line. I had a steep learning curve before me. I had never had a shower in my life before. The only place I'd been with indoor plumbing was at Grandpa Keay's on my Christmas holidays and there was certainly no shower in his house. There was only one washroom for the entire squad and that meant absolutely no privacy. You showered ten at a time, fought for a toilet and for the limited wash basins. The mirrors were only flat one directional ones on the wall and when you shaved you often had two guys trying to use the same mirror at the same time. This led to a lot of jostling and pushing going on with someone trying to establish dominance. We were issued with two towels, one hand towel and a bath towel, but no face cloth. This was hard on me as I was used to washing with a facecloth. The solution was to use one end of the face towel for washing the other to dry. Things settled down after a couple of weeks as you soon learned to survive by cooperating and working together. You made friends with like-minded members and stuck together. Harry Armstrong and I had side-by-side beds throughout our entire training and remained friends for all of our lives. He had worked in the Forestry industry before joining up and no one pushed him around.

I think my shy and timid nature must have been noted by the instructors early on as I got picked on more than my fair share of the time. One drill instructor, Sgt. Griffiths seemed to have a particular delight in singling me out for ridicule, be it my stance, my shoes, my uniform, my Sam Brown... one time he even claimed to find shaving cream behind my ear. He may have been right, but how the hell was I to know if there was shaving cream behind my ear. I didn't need to shave every morning and with the damn mirrors you couldn't see behind your ears anyway. I suffered through a lot of shame and embarrassment that first month with my friends assuring me that I was being picked on and not to worry. Easy for them to say.

I did alright in classes as I was a good listener and most of the tests they gave us were multiple-choice. I soon found that I had better memory than most and used this to my advantage staying in the top 4 or 5 of the class throughout both First and Second Class training. I lost out in the written work but made up for in Equitation. Having grown up on a farm and being around horses was a definite advantage when it came to being a "mounted policeman." In Rockcliffe we only got to ride for an hour every second day or so, but riding was still my salvation. Most of the squad had never been near a horse before and that's where the farm boys had the advantage and we made the most of it. Staff Sergeant (S/Sgt.) Anderson was the riding master and gave me hell for the way I rode but I never got bucked off or fell off on my own.

I got another break when it came time to issue us with breeches and riding boots. There were two of us that could not be fitted from the QM stores. I was too tall and skinny for the breeches they had, and the other guy was literally too big for his boots. His leg calves were as big as my waist. We ended up with the duty driver taking us down to the main RCMP tailor in Ottawa to be custom fitted for our breeches. The only material the tailor had was the lightweight officer's material and we ended up with much softer, lighter pair of breeches than what the rest of the squad were issued. I wore those breeches for nearly five years before I finally had to get them replaced.

I had two other run-ins with Sgt. Griffiths, one not so good and one a real surprise. The first was, again, on my Sam Brown not being polished enough to meet his liking. Foot drill was the last class of the day and once more he singled me out for another lecture; although friends said my kit was as good as any and better than some. I had reached the breaking point, threw my Sam Brown on the bed and declared that I was going out to get drunk. I had never even had so much as a beer in my life before, so I had no idea what I was talking about. However, I soon had no shortage of company and right after supper about eight of us headed down to the Chateau Laurier, the nicest hotel in Ottawa. This was a favourite recruits' drinking hole. We were all underage, but no one bothered us as they knew we were RCMP recruits by our haircut. We were well into our party when somebody noticed, *who else*, but Sgt. Griffiths sitting all alone in a dark corner keeping an eye on us. We didn't order any more drinks and made sure we were back in the Barracks before lights out. I never touched my Sam Brown and next morning we started off with Foot Drill as was the usual custom. Sgt. Griffiths in his daily inspection looked me up and down for a long time and then said, "Nice to see some improvement in your kit." I thought, "You SOB it's just a game you're playing. I'm as good as anyone else and you are not going to break me."

The next incident with Sgt. Griffiths involves a driving lesson. Everyone had to take driving lessons and we had a stupid driving instructor. We would go out for a half day with two recruits and the instructor. When my turn came up, I went out with another prairie boy called Ray Broberg. Rockcliffe was on the east side of Ottawa but we could not possibly start our driving lessons there. The driving instructor drove us through Ottawa across the bridge into Hull, Quebec and up into the Gatineau hills to a little roadside Cafe. We had a coffee while he went into the back with his lady friend/operator and from the giggling that went on I presume he got more than coffee.

Neither of us got a chance to start our driving until about 10:30 and by then we were on a narrow gravel road. The instructor claimed to know all the shortcuts to get us back to civilization and we kept on driving until we came to a bridge out. No one in their right mind would try to cross but he laid some planks over the holes and took over driving. To show off he went speeding off the far end, the car bounced up in the air, came down with a thud and stopped. He had landed on a rock, drove the oil pan into the flywheel and our driving was over. We walked all afternoon until we reached civilization and a phone booth. It took us several more hours for the tow truck to recover the car, find a way out and haul us all back to Rockcliffe.

We didn't get in until around lights out at 10.30 p.m. and the night NCO (non-commissioned officer) was none other than our old friend Sgt. Griffiths. He wanted to know where we had been and what happened. We wasted no time in telling him everything about that dumb stupid driving instructor and where we had been all day. His response was stated as a matter-of-fact, "Well he won't be driving anymore." His demeanour then switched completely, and the conversation went something like this:

"Have you had any dinner?" No.

"Any supper?" No.

"Well you boys go get cleaned up and get back here as soon as possible. I'll see if I can find something for you to eat."

We came right back down and there he was with his Sam Brown off, his tunic hanging on a chair, his shirt sleeves rolled up and he was whistling away over the kitchen range. He cooked up two of the biggest steaks we had ever seen along with some onions and refried potatoes. He gave us the choice of tea or coffee, served us and then sat down at the table to chat like an uncle or an old friend. He wanted to know all about our families, where we were from and if we were writing home to our mothers. We finished off with a piece of pie and then he reverted to his old self, "Now get on up to bed and don't turn the lights on." There was only one light switch for the entire room and since it was after "Lights out" he didn't want us waking everybody up.

I think that with the wisdom that comes with age most of us realized that those crabby old bastards in training were just doing their jobs. They were making boys into men and preparing us for the life ahead. They were making us into policemen who would uphold and maintain the reputation of the Royal Canadian Mounted Police, an envious reputation that had been established over the past 75 years. This was not always going to be an easy way of life and we had better be prepared for the trials and tribulations which lay before us.

Our squad graduated from our First Part training during Christmas week. By then we were all fitted with our Red Serge and given the rest of our kit, long blue dress slacks with the yellow stripe and our Wellington boots with box spurs. I don't remember much about the graduation, but we were all looking forward to the New

Year's Eve celebration. Some of the recruits that were from nearby may have gotten home for the holidays, but 90% of us were staying in barracks over Christmas and New Year's. The New Year's banquet and ball was organized by the staff, but the recruits all had to chip in a few dollars towards the party.

We changed our drill hall into a beautifully decorated ballroom complete with the traditional rotating mirror ball hanging from the ceiling, with spotlights shining on it for mood effect. Best of all was the importing of several busloads of young ladies from the local hospitals and universities. This was apparently a yearly occurrence and looked forward to by the local girls. There was no picking and choosing, the girls came by, took your arm and you had a date for the night. I think we got two beers each for the night and there was no hard liquor. Photographs were taken of each couple and some of my friends were kind enough to send mine to my mother without my knowledge. I discovered it on my first visit home. There I was with my eyes glossy and I looked half pickled. Mum was kind enough to say that my date was certainly a nice-looking young lady. I don't remember her name and never corresponded or heard from her again. After the party was over the recruits, with staff supervision, stripped the drill hall in about an hour and everything was back to normal for the morning parade.

On January 2, 1948 our Squad 42 boarded the train in Ottawa and we were shipped off to "Depot" Division in Regina, where we became "A" Troop. We arrived in the middle of a blizzard and were assigned to the third floor of "C" Block, the very place where I'd slept through the Commissioner's inspection. The building was so old and drafty that snow crept through the windows, doors and every crack possible. We had to make up our beds with cold bedding and it was a rough night for some of those who had never slept in a cold house before. I had "come home" and was smart enough to sleep that first night in my long johns. Even with all the clothes we owned piled on top of us it was a cold night and a rude welcome to "Depot" Division.

In Regina (Depot Division) we took what was called Part II Training and it was a lot more enjoyable and instructive than Rockcliffe. We were now getting into more investigative training and with the Crime Lab on site we had good instructors as well as access to the crime lab itself. We still did a lot of marching but also had lessons on boxing, wrestling, police holds, making arrests, typing reports, attending court and the handling of documents, etc. I believe that all told we had over forty subjects in our training curriculum. There was also the indoor swimming pool where you learned to swim if you wanted to or not. We could use the pool on our own after hours and lots of us non-swimmers got in extra practise just for the fun of it. As the senior troop we were also exposed to our first "duty shifts" when we were assigned to evening guard duty. This was on the gate to see that only authorized people were on the premises and that the recruits were back before bedtime. This was all under the supervision of an NCO.

My best memories of Regina were the riding, or equitation, as it was called. Soon after arriving in Regina it was established that we were going to be the first musical ride troop after the war. This was looked upon by most of us as a once-in-a-lifetime adventure. It would be much more exciting to go on tour, represent Canada's finest, see the world and be chased by beautiful young ladies than to be an ordinary Mountie. It didn't work out quite that way even for the ones that stayed on the ride.

Most of the ride horses were older than we were and had been out on pasture at Fort Walsh for the past six or seven years. There was no musical ride during the war. If the non-riders thought the Rockcliffe horses were a challenge, they had some new lessons to learn in Regina. If you were timid or couldn't ride those old horses sensed it immediately and you soon found yourself bucked off and laying in the dirt. The riding master in Regina was an older S/Sgt. by the name of Cecil Walker. He and I got along fine and I was frequently called upon to ride particularly frisky or misbehaving horses. We had a rough rider, Cst. George Cuttings, but he only rode horses that needed special training. When George retired, he ended up with the Edmonton Veterans Division and continued to ride well into his 90s. We attended many of the same RCMP Veterans' AGM's and we always had time for a visit and a story or two. When we got into serious musical ride training, I started out as a section leader of eight horses. Before long I was moved up to lead rider of all 32 horses. We tried several horses for the leader to get one that was constant in all paces - walk, trot and canter. I finally ended up with a horse called "Peter." He was a beautiful easy horse to ride and seemed to know all the ride movements as well as I did.

All was going well with my classes and I felt I was finally on a par with everyone else in the Troop. By early summer we were riding outside for at least two hours a day. We were also riding into the city, including one parade, to get the horses used to noise and pavement. As the senior Troop we had certain privileges and as the lead rider I finally felt respected by my colleagues. Life was good and we were looking forward to opening the ride in New York's Madison Square Gardens in about five weeks' time. All that changed on a Friday afternoon when eleven of us were called into the OCs office. Some idiot in Ottawa had decided we were too young to be Canadian ambassadors abroad. The eleven of us were to be sent out into the field and senior men were to be brought in for the ride. They picked every second man until they had eleven. Why that number and why wait until five weeks before the ride was to go on tour, no one ever knew. The Riding Master was never consulted on the members to be selected and from the reactions in Depot Division, I don't think anyone else was either. S/Sgt. Walker didn't know anything about this until we told him in the stables on Saturday morning. He was one mad distraught Riding Master and I never had the pleasure of saying goodbye or ever seeing him again. My good friend Harry Armstrong moved up to take my place as lead rider and never left the ride. He spent his full 35 years with the horses in Regina or Ottawa and retired as Riding Master with the rank of S/Sgt. He also got to present several RCMP horses to the Queen, starting with Burmese in 1969 at the Royal Windsor Horse Show in London.

Graduation of "A" Troop, Regina 1948

Time at "K" Division Headquarters

On Monday Cst. Ray Broberg and I caught the train for Edmonton and on Tuesday I was officially a member of "K" Division RCMP, where I spent my entire twenty-six years of service. In training it was suggested that we would likely be posted to the neighbouring province as we would not be sent to our home area. I was quite happy going to Alberta rather than Manitoba, but I was most unhappy about being pulled off the ride. With our early departure there was no formal graduation or even a party to say goodbye to our colleagues with whom we had been bonding for the last ten months.

There were about 25 single members in Edmonton, and we had our own men's mess. There was one big bedroom and one small one (Room 213B) with three beds, which I was lucky enough to get. The bathrooms hadn't changed much over Regina so there was not much difference in living accommodation. I was just another kid recruit and had to start earning my way up from the bottom. Two of the first members I remember meeting in Edmonton were Csts. Bob Wood and Art Devlin. They were confined to barracks for some minor misdemeanour and I got to visit with them in the evening. Bob Wood had a girlfriend by the name of June Koluk. Her parent's home was a meeting place for all Edmonton single members. Bob and June married and spent most of their service overseas on Security and Immigration. After retirement Bob returned to Calgary and was Chief of Security for Alberta Government Telephones (TELUS.) We reconnected when I was with RBC and they became part of our Gourmet Dinner Club. Curly & Helen Elliott, Bob &

June Wood, Ralph & Vivian Toews, Dennis & Jean Norton and Jack & Edna Kenny comprised the Gourmet Club. Each couple catered one gourmet dinner a year and it has gone on for over thirty years. Unfortunately, Jack and Edna are the only couple left. I have known June longer than any other female in my life, with the exception of my sister Margaret.

To get back to my story, it was in the Edmonton Division Mess that I picked up my damn "Curly" nickname. About 30 of us were having dinner when a loud obnoxious member came in and shouted, "Hey Curly." I turned around to see who he was, and he pointed his finger at me, laughed and continued with his Curly bit. When I was young and had hair it was wavy, but not curly and it was Cst. Gordon Stratton who was the subject of his gesture. Some of the other members picked up the taunt and it continued on the next day. I didn't stop it at the time and the rest is history. I've tried a thousand times since to go back to my real name - but once you are stuck with something like that – you are stuck. Gordon Stratton ended up being best man at our wedding.

The first recruit posting in Edmonton was often the guard room which is of course where I started my policing career. We had cells with prisoners who had to be guarded, prisoners and mental patients to be escorted and someone had to attend Superior Courts in Red serge. I often got the court detail. I didn't understand the intricacies of questioning witnesses and was bored with the lawyers asking the same dumb question over and over again and getting the same answer from the witness. My first wakeup call came when I went to sleep sitting with the prisoner and the judge sent his clerk down to shake me awake. I didn't do that again. We escorted most of our prisoners, both male and female, to Oliver or Fort Saskatchewan. Cst. Cecil Coombs drove the paddy wagon and Mrs. Cottrell was the Matron - and not to be trifled with.

They were a real pair of characters to work with and taught me a lot about escorting and life in general. We were also tasked with the job of moving mental patients from Edmonton to the psychiatric hospital in Ponoka. For this we used an old Air Force ambulance which was no more than a one-ton truck with a large windowless box on the back. The seats were benches down both sides and across the front. Comfort was not an option. Why they needed Police to escort sick people I'll never know. Most of the women were middle-aged and were no crazier than any of us but were merely having troubles with normal mid-life changes. On the way back the three of us would cram into the cab of the truck, race back to Edmonton and our day would be over by 2:00 o'clock. This left me with nothing to do and I started going out with the guys on Highway Patrol. I remember writing my first traffic ticket which was on No. 2 Highway just south of Edmonton at a place called Ellerslie. This was both a high accident area and a school zone which was a good place for tickets. We chased down and stopped a car with four occupants and the fellows told me, "Go write the ticket." I - shaking and scared stiff, filled in all the blanks until I came to the one which asked for occupation. The reluctant driver finally admitted they were all teachers, on the way to a Principals meeting and should have known better than speed through a school zone.

Most of my solo escort trips were to either Vancouver or the Prince Albert Penitentiary. On all out of province trips we were required to wear Red Serge. Vancouver was the worst as it was by train and overnight coming back to Edmonton. You got an upper berth on the way out and arrived in Vancouver early in the morning. You then spent the day on paperwork and picking up your prisoner. The train left Vancouver in the early evening and didn't get into Edmonton until noon the next day. This meant you were up for 36 hours and had to be awake with your wits about you at all times. The Prince Albert trip was easier as you left about 8:00 in the evening and arrived in Saskatoon about 4:00 AM. You then walked your prisoner(s) over to the city cells and locked them up for a few hours. This gave you a chance to get an hour or so of sleep, wash up, have breakfast and then make the hour and a half run up to Prince Albert. On a number of occasions, I was able to arrange the timing of the escorts so I could have a weekend in Paddockwood.

The only prisoner I escorted of note was Ronald Victor Stanley. He was a professional safe blower and specialized in blowing rural elevator safes. He had been convicted a number of times, resulting in penitentiary sentences. After his last conviction there were long and protracted legal arguments over whether or not he should be declared a habitual criminal. In the end the Crown won out and he was the first Canadian to receive that designation. This meant that he had an indeterminate sentence and could be held in the penitentiary as long as the authorities decided. I think every member in Edmonton warned me about escorting him. I was advised to keep him in handcuffs, leg irons, plus ball & chain and never take my eyes off him for one minute as he would undoubtedly make a break for freedom. When it came time to escort him, we sat together, and he turned out to be one of the most interesting crooks that I'd ever had the pleasure of taking to jail.

He explained that when you do a crime and don't get caught, it gives you a big thrill and you think you're invincible. You keep it up until you're caught and end up in jail. Crime was just a game and you continued with your illegal activities until it became a way of life. Sometimes you win and sometimes you lose, and he lost big-time. He didn't think it was the best way to get his name into the history books. When I finished with my transfer within the penitentiary, he shook my hand and wished me well in my career. Gentlemen come in all stripes.

On September 1st, 1948 the Force changed the pension plan from Part 111 to Part V. I stayed under Part 111, which was not really a smart move, but worked out OK in the end. At the same time, they changed the underage recruit designation from a Recruit Special Constable to three designations with starting ranks, of Constable Third, Second and First class. To accomplish this, they resorted to the usual government bureaucratic overkill and forced all of us under 21 to officially resign. All the paperwork was done on August 26th, 1948 and then I had to reapply filling out - in my own handwriting - the same application form I had submitted in the fall of 1946. We all had to take our Oath of Allegiance and Oath of Office over again to be effective August 31st, 1948. That is when I got my proper regimental number #15338. Both the resignation and the re-engagement were published in General Orders which went out all across Canada. I was promoted to Constable Second Class on September 1, 1950 and I presume to First Class on the same date 1951. Anyone who was over 21 when they joined got their regimental number immediately, more pay and were always deemed to be a head of us for promotions. No one ever said life in the Force was fair or even and you worked for everything you got.

I think because I was always Mum's helper that Grandpa Keay took a particular interest in me and was pleased with my career choice. I received a postcard from him in December 1948 and have kept it for over 65 years. Why I don't know, except it is a reminder of what a truly wonderful Grandpa he was. The post card read in part "All very pleased to hear of your doings. Hope that you will get out this way sometime." At that time Grandpa was living in Port Alberni with his daughter, my Aunt May and her husband Bram Vanderkracht.

In the fall of 1949 I took grandpa up on his invitation. Cst. Ralph Toews and I took the train to Vancouver and the ferry across to Victoria. Ralph had friends there and I stayed a few days with my Uncle Chick. I went up to Port Alberni on my own. That is where I got involved with another one of my little adventures. Grandpa had a homemade wooden boat with a little lawn mower motor in it which we used for salmon trolling in the Alberni harbour. There were lots of salmon, but we were not catching any and Grandpa decided we should go down the channel to some bay where the Chinook salmon were gathered. To do this he called upon the kindness of a ham radio operator friend who had a larger boat complete with a small cabin. He was about Grandpa's age and had only one arm. The salmon were cooperating, and we ended up with two nice 30 plus pound salmon.

After we had our salmon they decided to stop and see an old friend of theirs who had a cabin along the channel. It was supposedly for a coffee, but a bottle of scotch materialized from somewhere and the glasses were filled. Stories were told, laughter was shared, and we didn't start for home till well after dark. He had a small light on the front of his boat, and all was going well until we got right into the harbour at Port Alberni. There we ran into an illegal fishing net strung across the harbour and tied to one of the marker poles. We cut the motor and should have slid over it but what we didn't know was that the steel keel strip on his boat had come loose and we snagged the net. We were hung up and could go neither forward nor back off. We tried everything and, in the end, decided we had to cut our way out of the net. I stripped down to my underwear, they tied a rope around me, and I started hacking away at the net while they held me by the heels. We got the top line of the net cut on both sides but still couldn't get the boat loose. I ended up going further and further underwater. The knife had no lanyard so I had to hold on to it and every time I tried to cut the net another fish would hit the net and jerk it out of my hand. I was not a happy camper. We must have cut a 25- or 30-foot chunk out of the net and when we finally got loose and the net on board, we had 10 or so nice Spring Salmon in the boat. At the dock Grandpa phoned Uncle Bram and told him to come down with a gunny sack.

He gave Grandpa hell for worrying them so much until he saw our load of fish and heard our story and then he was quite happy. As a young policeman I was worried that the illegal poachers would recognize the boat and do some harm. Nothing happened but I've often wondered what would've happened if I had got tangled in that net underwater and if two old men with three arms between them would have been enough to pull me out. Household refrigerators were not normal in 1949 so whenever Grandpa caught a fish, he usually shared it with his neighbours. The next morning after our bountiful harvest he was dropping off whole fish with the warning, "Don't ask and don't tell." He was a true Scotchman.

I was transferred from the Guard Room to Highway Patrol sometime in the early spring of 1949. Our boss was Sgt. Jimmy Muir. He was a little guy, too short for RCMP standards but joined the Force when the Alberta Provincial Police were absorbed in 1932. He was not popular with his men and was detested by every trucker in Alberta. Notwithstanding that Highway Patrol was a lot of fun when you were young. We had one Senior Constable and the rest of us were basically Recruits just starting out. We had radio contact but once you left the office you were on your own. We worked two members per car and usually had two shifts working days and evenings. We worked opposite directions out of the city but would team up for serious accidents. My first contact with moving dead bodies came early.

We couldn't get married for seven years after joining the force, so no one had any serious girlfriends and we were a pretty happy cohesive group. This all came to a sudden end one Friday afternoon when I was minding my own business and quietly resting in my bedroom, which was directly over where Sgt. Muir parked his patrol car. I heard a crash outside the window and saw that my Sergeant had just backed his patrol car right into the side of an unmarked vehicle exiting the post garage. I grabbed up my camera and snapped a couple of pictures before he had time to move the vehicle. Half the people in the building heard the crash so the buzz soon went around that Sgt. Muir had just backed into a General Investigation Service (GIS) vehicle. Word also got around that Cst. Elliott had pictures of the accident before the Sgt. had time to move his vehicle. The film was arbitrarily seized, developed and proved three things: Firstly - that the Sgt. for whom I worked was in the wrong; secondly – Sergeants have no sense of humour; and thirdly my services were required in Peace River, immediately.

I was never questioned about the accident and the taking of pictures could not have affected it in any way. Working with or under Sgt. Muir may have been awkward for a while but I did nothing wrong and once again I was left feeling unfairly treated. On Saturday morning I was called into the Sergeant Major's (S/Ms) office and informed that I was being transferred to Peace River Sub/Division by RCMP aircraft on Monday morning at 8.00 a.m. No questions, no explanation, no appeal - just shut up and go. This was an unscheduled flight and I was the only person on our Beechcraft twin engine airplane. The pilots were as unhappy as I was and on arriving in Peace River, they didn't even bother to shut down the port engine. I was unceremoniously dumped onto the tarmac with my trunk and the aircraft was on its way back to Edmonton. I have tried to sell the theory that on account of that one historic flight the aircraft was declared a national treasure and is now mounted on a pedestal in front of the museum at "Depot" Division in Regina. The plane is located there but not too many have bought into my story.

The RCMP aircraft that flew me to Peace River

Peace River Days

As soon as possible after arriving in Peace River I was paraded before the O.C., Inspector (Insp.) Frank Spalding. He was obviously not expecting me and had no immediate position in mind so informed me that I could start off that afternoon on Town Detail. I was given a key and when I inquired about a ride, I was informed that "This is Peace River, you walk." It was only a short walk downtown so walking was no problem. However, it was rather embarrassing to have to stop strangers and explain that you were new in town and could they please tell you where the police station was located. I found the office alright and prayed that no one would come in and ask me any questions. I spent the afternoon reading Rules & Regulations, old files, and discovering more bylaws, statutes and criminal laws than I ever imagined existed. Fortunately, not a soul came in to bother me so at 5:00 o'clock I locked up and walked back to Head Quarters. A new stage in my life and career had begun.

Friday of that week was November 11th, and Remembrance Day. I had not been assigned any duties, had today off and was standing outside when this old guy dressed in red arrived in a beat-up English Anglia car. I was not interested in the old guy, but I sure did have eyes for his beautiful young female chauffeur. Her name was Helen and the old guy was Reg. # 6681, Cst. Francis Daniel (D.F.) Atkins – who would become my future father-in-law. Getting unceremoniously shunted off to Peace River was turning out to be not so bad after all.

It didn't take too long in Peace River before I realized that although it was still a quasi- military organization it was much more relaxed than either of the training Depots or "K" Division headquarters in Edmonton. You didn't argue or question too much but at least you could discuss things and the Non-Commissioned Officers were leaders rather than just bosses. Peace River Sub/Division covered a huge area from Smith (Smith Landing in 1949) north to the Northwest Territories boundary, west to British Columbia's border and to the Athabasca River on the east. In this whole area there were only about 45 RCMP members in total. That is about equal to the size of Cochrane Detachment in 2016.

This is the area I would become very familiar with over the next 10 years. The senior personnel in Peace River were:

- Inspector Frank Spalding O.C. Sub/Division
- Staff Sergeant Ernie Hertzogg, S/Div. NCO
- Staff Sergeant Harry Wickstrom, I/C Peace River Detachment
- Sergeant Carl Doey, 2/I/C Detachment
- Corporal Doug Banting, S/Div. reader
- Constable D.F. "Frank" Atkins, Provost

There were also two Csts. with fixed positions. One was the Dog Master and the second was the Identification specialist. We had one Senior Cst. and the other eight or nine of us were brand-new with less than four years' service.

In the basement of the subdivision headquarters building there were cells for about 10 prisoners, and it was officially classified as a provincial jail. This accounts for Cst. Frank Atkins being the Provost. We only took trustee prisoners who were serving a sentence of three months or less. The prisoners' meals were provided by Ma Rinder, who ran a boarding house right next to the police property. She had been doing this for years - too many years. The meals were wholesome and plentiful, but hygiene was sometimes not her forte. Most of the prisoners were Native and getting better meals then at home so no one complained.

There was seldom serious crime anywhere in the Peace River country in the 1950s. Illicit drugs were unheard of; guns were used for hunting and murders happened only on very rare occasions. Most criminal offences were petty theft or the odd break and entry into a rural store. Most of our time was spent on Provincial matters or social assistance. Open possession of liquor in public places was a common offence and took up a lot of our time. Illegal drinking around rural dance halls was very prevalent and police were present at the dances as often as the orchestra. Although people undoubtedly drove with more alcohol in their system than is allowed at the present time, drunk driving was a difficult offence to prove in court and so it was deemed easier just to take away their liquor in the first place. People developed ingenious ways of trying to hide their booze and it was a bit of a cat and mouse game finding it, but no one took it too seriously. It was only a $25 fine but involved a court appearance and took up a lot of our time.

There was no official single men's dining mess in Peace River. With 10 or so single men always coming and going we had our own unofficial mess. This worked fairly well with everyone helping out with the cooking and funding their share of the grocery costs. The pots, pans and dishes were all hand me downs but were enough for us. We had a large garden which the prisoners attended all summer. This provided us with fresh vegetables and the trustee prisoners were also willing to wash dishes for a package or two of cigarettes. In the fall we had several geese and duck hunters on staff and the prisoners were experts at cleaning these birds up for us. We never had much baking or desserts until another farm boy from Saskatchewan by the name of Ed Glasser showed up. With raspberries and saskatoons free for the picking, pies were suddenly on the menu. His mother had taught him to make pies and he turned out to be a pretty good cook. Needless to say, he was one of the more popular members.

With all the single members and the nurses' residents being only a block and a half away, needless to say there was considerable socializing going on. By a strange coincidence the key to the police building also fit the main door of the nurses' residence, a great asset for bypassing the Matron and the nurses coming in after hours. Oddly enough the key to the Grande Prairie detachment office also worked in the nurse's residence at that point. It seems there must have been a romantic matchmaker either in the building trade or in the RCMP long before I arrived.

I had no interest in nurses as I had already set my sights on Helen. Unfortunately, it was a well-known fact that she was not going to get "scarlet fever" and marry any Mounted Policeman. She was certainly a very popular young lady, in our social group but she was playing the field and doing things her way. I did not take her to the New Year's dance but her date either got overly friendly or intoxicated and I ended up walking her home. I thought that such a gallant gesture by a fine gentleman like myself should warrant a good night kiss, however, instead I got the screen door slammed in my face. That only proved beyond all doubt that she was my kind of a girl and the challenge for her hand was on.

My first winter in Peace River was one of the coldest ever recorded. It was continuously below -45C for over 40 days. The police dog was moved into the garage, so we couldn't keep a car running inside but had one running outside for 24 hours a day. Around March we started receiving Alberta Motor Association (AMA) pamphlets requesting assistance in setting up a school patrol in Peace River. No one paid much attention to these until one morning Cst. Don Kirk and I were assigned to get into our Red Serge and be at the school that afternoon to set up this new school safety program. Don had a lower regimental number than I, was a senior man and I presumed that he would be making the presentation. Driving down we got into a heated argument over this and it became apparent that Don was petrified over standing up in front of a class of kids and I would be the one doing the talking. The only good part of this was that Miss Helen Atkins was the Grade V1 teacher. I was wishing I had paid more attention to those AMA instruction books!

I arrived in the classroom with not a clue as to what I was going to say or how it was going to get started. I solved this by walking slowly back and forth across the classroom as the children would do in a crosswalk. I stopped, turned to face the students and said, "How would you like me for a teacher, better than Ms. Atkins I'll bet." Of course, the children all clapped and hollered, and I had their attention but the look on Helen's face let me know that I'd stepped over the boundaries of her good affections. I was familiar with school patrols from my days on Highway Patrol around Edmonton and the surrounding area. I dwelt on what I had seen, assuring them that the police and the school administration would help and that they would have a very important job, keeping the younger students safe. It all seemed to work OK and by the time class was over I had a bunch of excited and enthusiastic kids.

Helen and I

After my opening remarks I was sure that Helen could not possibly refuse my apology. She accepted my offer and we walked down to the McNamara Hotel for a coffee. The children of members, no matter what their age, were not allowed to ride in marked police cars. After coffee I walked Helen the rest of the way home and that was our first date. After a few more coffee dates, the odd movie night, bike rides and tennis matches, we were seeing each other quite often. By the end of the summer Helen had somewhat relented on her – "I am not marrying a damn Mounted Policeman" bit – and we were becoming best friends. I think I was unwittingly helped along in my quest by Helen's mother Sarah, who in my esteem was the best mother-in-law anyone could possibly wish for. It came to my attention through Jeanie, Helen's sister, that Sarah had backed Helen into a corner and said – "When are you ever going to smarten up and realize that the best-looking men don't make the best husbands." I have been forever in her debt for that little bit of parental advice.

I don't remember any outstanding cases or special investigations while I was at Peace River. There were certainly none that I was involved in. There was a murder on a remote Indian Reserve which required the charter of a floatplane to take the investigators to the scene. They were able to use the aircraft's radio to advise that the prisoner was a female and a matron would be necessary on their return. The Officer Commanding (O.C.) at the time was Insp. K. Shakespeare and he insisted on being there to meet the plane, like he was going to solve the crime or something, but all he could talk about was that beautiful young matron - and who was she? The answer was "That's Frank's daughter, Helen." The guys all had a good laugh and Helen probably got paid all of $.25 an hour.

That same spring I was assigned to treaty paying duty. Ever since Treaty No. 7 was signed at Gleichen, Alberta in 1877, the Indigenous Peoples of Canada have been paid treaty money as per their treaty agreements. The Chiefs got $25.00 and the rest $5.00 each per year. Not a lot of money now but a sizeable payment a hundred years ago. The money was paid out once a year by the area "Indian Agent." An RCMP member always had to be present at the ceremony. In many cases the Natives would only take the money from the "Red Coat" because the Indian Agent was not trusted. For which in many cases there was ample justification.

We flew around in a Norseman floatplane, and as was usually the case, it was grossly overloaded. Besides the pilot, Indian Agent and myself, there would be an x-ray technician, dentist, probably a doctor and maybe at least one Ottawa bureaucrat who was on a summer paid adventure. Add to that we had to have an electricity generator, x-ray

equipment, darkroom/tent, dental equipment, plus their supplies, the agency records of every Indian in the area and of course a bunch of cash. If we were staying overnight, add to that the sleeping bags and our personal grooming kits. All the heavy items were loaded on first then you crawled in and lay down or sat where you could find a soft spot. The last person held the door shut while we took off. Only the pilot and the Indian Agent had seats. On one trip the agent's secretary came with us and even he had to ride in the back.

The treaty money was paid at about the same time and in the same place each year, usually at a Hudson's Bay or a free trader's post. The Indians would be waiting on our arrival so the first thing to do was to set up the x-rays and dental stations. Tuberculosis (TB) was rampant in the north at that time so the plan was to have all adults x-rayed before they got their money. The dentist would concentrate on the younger people who still had some teeth left. All births, deaths, and marriages were also recorded. When it came to handing out the money the agent would count it out, hand it to me, I would count it again and hand it over to the recipient. Sometimes if I didn't count it they would just stand there until I did. They wanted assurance from the trusty Mountie that their amount was correct. We always had to take some $1.00 bills as some of the older women would not take the $5.00 bill believing that five one-dollar bills was more money.

I was transferred to Slave Lake Detachment in August 1950, but the next spring I was again detailed for treaty paying duties. This time the float plane was a 1935 Waco by-plane. It resembled something right out of WWI, smaller but hauled just as much as the Norseman. I don't remember all the remote places we visited but starting from the south end some of them would have been Calling Lake, Wabasca, Atikameg (White Fish Lake) Trout Lake, Peerless Lake, Loon Lake and Cadotte Lake. We were also able to go by car to such places as Slave Lake, Grouard and Sturgeon Lake. By the time I was done paying treaty I was fairly familiar with the area that would be my workplace for the next ten years. I only had one testy encounter while paying treaty and that was at Calling Lake when an enterprising pilot with his own aircraft arrived with a load of pop and ice cream.

He was selling them for $1.00 each (four or five times the going rate) and was taking money from the Indians as fast as we were paying it out. This didn't sit well with the local trading company who needed that money to cover their debts. Although the guy was cheating the Indians, he was not doing anything wrong and there was nothing I could do about it. The local trader was so worked up that he was threatening to put a bullet hole through the aircraft engine. I assured him that if he damaged the aircraft in any way or assaulted the pilot, he would be getting a free ride back to Slave Lake. The situation resolved itself when the pop ran out and the ice cream started to melt.

Slave Lake was a three single member detachment with Cpl. Gordon Bligh in charge. It was a log building with no inside facilities and very few comfort features. The Detachment area covered from Smith on the south east to the Driftpile Reserve on the west end, a total of about 80 miles of gravel road. Other than north to Wabasca there was very little activity outside of policing along the highway. This was still part of the Alaska Highway route and there were always lots of US citizens going to or coming from Alaska. To say that most of them were stupid and ill prepared for northern travel would be treating them kindly. Consequently, accidents were some of our biggest problems. There were still US army convoys coming through and even they created problems with rollovers and abandoned vehicles.

Slave Lake Detachment

Winter road on a good day

I was fortunate in Slave Lake to have been adopted by the Gunnar Wahlstrom family. They were big in the lumbering industry and owned or operated several small bush saw mills. They also had boys about my age, and I think we were supposed to influence each other. Another family that took pity on me was the Troutman's who owned and operated the only garage and car dealership in town. I bought my first car from them, a 1935 Chevrolet Coupe. I didn't keep that car too long as they switched me over to a 1947 Plymouth four-door sedan which was much newer and nicer. This car was a beauty to drive, took Helen and I to Saskatchewan in 1951, on our honeymoon in 1952 and we finally sold it in 1953 to finance our first house in Grand Prairie.

I had two police car accidents during my short stay at Slave Lake Detachment – not a good start for future postings. The first was on October 10th, 1950. The O.C. had mandated that every Detachment in the Sub/Division do one-night patrol per week and he sent out the schedule. This meant that you may have been out on an accident or other investigation until 3.00 in the morning, but that night you did another patrol from 8.00 p.m., to 4.00 a.m. Cpl. Bligh was on leave and that left Cst. Norm Goodfellow and I to hold fort. At about 2.00 a.m., we were heading back towards Canyon Creek with me driving and Norm sleeping. I could see the lights of an all-night café and was looking forward to a coffee when I fell asleep, crossed the road and ran into a brush pile in the left ditch. I had to pay $14.68, 25% of the repair costs, about a week's wages at that time. Norm was paraded and given a severe reprimand for being the senior man and asleep on duty. He was not a detachment man and soon went back to a 9.00 to 5.00 desk job in Edmonton.

In the winter of 1949/50 Shell Oil was doing a lot of oil exploration north of Slave Lake all the way up to Red Earth. This meant that for the first time ever we were able to use the winter ice roads to reach some of the more remote settlements. Over the Christmas holidays there was a break-in at the Peerless Lake store and the two culprits were identified by the time we got the complaint. We only had a Justice of the Peace at Slave Lake and since break & entry was an indictable offence, we required a Magistrate to hold court. Our closest Magistrate was Joe Bissell in High Prairie. Joe had been in the RCMP, won a $28.000 Irish Sweepstake in 1928 and took up farming. He was a good Magistrate with a lot of common sense. When trying to set a date for a trial and knowing of the winter roads he suggested that he'd like to see some of that area and that we should take court to the site of the offence. His rationale was that it would show the locals that they were not beyond the law, that the court would come to them and especially that the offenders were treated fairly.

On January 19th, Joe and I headed off to Wabasca, held court there on some minor stuff and stayed overnight at the Catholic Mission. Next day we arrived in Peerless Lake before noon and I'm sure it was the first car, not alone the first Police car, ever seen at that point. The two suspects were rounded up, admitted their crime and I established there was sufficient evidence to proceed with formal charges. The Information documents had been typed at Slave Lake and all I had to do was pen in the names. First thing we had to do was to find and swear in an impartial interpreter. I opened court and then became the prosecutor while Joe went to extra length to ensure everyone understood the proceedings. In the end he sentenced the bad guys to a few months in jail and everyone left happy. It was my first sole adventure at remote homegrown justice, and I was pretty pleased with myself for a 2/Class Cst. with just a year of policing experience.

We had the two prisoners in the back and were on our way home when an accident occurred. It was on a narrow bulldozed road winding its way through the bush. We were going around a hill and I had the downhill side when a Shell Oil truck came around the curve. I immediately turned into the right snowbank to get as far off the road as possible and was both stopped and stuck. The young fellow driving the truck panicked, put on his brakes and slid into my front fender. The prisoners laughed and thought that going to jail was lots of fun. I got pulled out, the car was still driveable so after collecting all the necessary information we continued on to Slave Lake. The senior Shell employee in the truck admitted their fault and assured me they would pay in full for the repairs. Not so simple in the Mounted Police force. This was my second accident in three months, and I think the O.C. had a desk job in mind for me. He instructed Cpl. Orville Poll, the NCO I/C. McLennan Detachment to *FULLY* investigate the accident, including photos of the accident scene. This involved a 110-mile trip to Slave Lake and another 75 miles to the accident site. He stopped in High Prairie and got a statement from Joe Bissell and even with that evidence the O.C. made him continue the investigation. He was away from his detachment for three days, leaving his single man with no transportation. He stayed in Slave Lake overnight when we got back from Peerless Lake. Next morning before he left, we checked our mail and had a cheque from Shell Oil, not only covering the $106.15 for car repair, but with additional funds for inconvenience and loss of use. I don't know who got the extra money – but it was not me. The reports eventually made their way to Ottawa and on February 26th, I got their reply clearing me from any fault. I never heard a word from the O.C.

The standard for all Detachment personnel at the time was one weekend off a month. The weekend didn't start until you had all your exhibit reports in from any Friday night's seizures and all other paperwork completed. You also required a pass

(Form F33) from the O.C. authorising you to leave your Detachment area. My weekends were always to Peace River to visit Helen. Frank and Sarah still had a wood stove and the joke was that every time I put in for a pass Frank ordered another load of wood. It was my job to split the wood – which I did on a regular basis. David Armstrong, Helen's sister's boyfriend at the time, cut his finger on his first try and was exempt from any future wood splitting. Helen would also ride the bus down to see me on weekends and stayed with the Municipal Health nurse who worked and lived next door to the Detachment.

At the end of February 1951, I was transferred from Slave Lake to High Prairie Detachment. This was a bit of an unusual move for an experimental policing trial that the O.C. had thought up. I was one of the few young single members with a car and had agreed to use it to set up a temporary Police presence in Valleyview. I was to spend three days a week in Valleyview, living and eating in the hotel and use my own vehicle for transportation. I got $.07 a mile from the time I left High Prairie until my return and all living expenses paid. The price of gas was around $.45 a gallon so I could pay off my car loan and cut my living expenses in half. There was a lot of oil drilling activity around Sturgeon Lake and the #34 highway was being built, starting from both ends, Valleyview and Whitecourt. This meant that there were lots of roughnecks around, but I soon found out that if I controlled the bar, I controlled the town. My biggest problem was with drunk Indians on the Sturgeon Lake Reserve. I had no place to lock them up and all I could do was take them home, handcuff them somewhere or dump them off in a remote location and hope they didn't get into trouble. My post in High Prairie was an exciting time, but also had a steep learning curve as I had less than two years of actual policing experience and was on my own no matter what situation came up. There was no radio communication and the phone service to my Cpl. Beggs in High Prairie was limited at the best of times. I had no office, typewriter or law books in Valleyview so had lots of extra typing and paperwork to do on top of my regular duties on my days back in High Prairie. Fortunately, there was always some local family who would look after us young RCMP Csts. In my case it was Bob and Kate Keller at Sturgeon Lake and the Eng family, a Scandinavian family, in High Prairie. The Kellers ran a cafe and summer resort while the Eng's owned a restaurant and bus stop in High Prairie and I was successful in recruiting their son Allen into the Force.

With the extra income from the use of my car and a reduction in my living expenses I was able to start saving up some money. It was a good thing as I had purchased a diamond engagement ring from the High Prairie Drug store. There were no jewellery stores at that time, but here again the friendly druggist brought in some samples and not only gave me a break on the price but let me pay for it in instalments. In August 1951 Helen and I made our first trip together to visit my folks in Paddockwood. I gave Helen her ring on the sandy beach at Waskesiu and we danced the night away in the famous Lake Side Ballroom before heading home. Next morning Mum didn't say anything about our engagement and by noon Helen was getting frantic over her lack of comment. I finally took Mum aside to find out what was wrong and found out nothing was wrong. She didn't know whether or not she had missed seeing the ring before and was too embarrassed to say anything. A little tip from her favourite son cleared that up and soon there were smiles and joy in abundance. Helen liked my Mum as much as I liked Sarah and I don't think there was ever an unfavourable mother-in-law comment throughout marriage.

We came home via Saskatoon and Helen wanted to "splurge", so we stayed in the Bessborough Hotel. When going through her scrapbooks researching for this history, I found that she still had the hotel receipts for our two rooms on which she had written "Posh but expensive." The rooms were $6.00 each – which was expensive when you are making about $2.00 a day. From Saskatoon we went to Irma, Alberta to visit her good friend Jean Larson. Jean, Helen and Louise Best took their one year of B.E. Teacher training together at the University of Alberta and on graduation all got rural schools in the Irma area. Jean married Allan Larson – the only eligible bachelor – while Helen and Louise moved on to find their mates elsewhere. The three girls stayed in touch all their lives, but unfortunately, I think Louise is the only one left. We have not kept in touch since Helen's passing.

When we got engaged the RCMP regulations still required seven years of service before you could get married. That meant that we had to wait another three years and I had some real serious discussions on whether or not I was going to wait that long or find another job. Both Helen and her mother were adamant that we wait. Fortunately, it was shortly after that the service time was reduced to five years. Too many members were leaving and there was a big scandal in Regina when it came to light that seven members were secretly married and living together. Their subsequent dismissal raised a huge backlash all across Canada which led to Ottawa finally coming to their senses. You still had to have $1,200 cash or equivalent, and the Commissioner's approval of both YOUR WIFE and your marriage before you could proceed.

Life at High Prairie Detachment settled into a pretty predictable routine. We had two junior Csts. and the NCO I/C Cpl. Harry Beggs. The Town had also hired their own Police Cst. Frank Brown. He had no policing background but became our unofficial fourth man and was a big help as he knew all the locals. I continued my three days a week at Valleyview, took my one weekend off a month and Helen came down to visit quite often. She had worked as a telephone operator and sometimes worked as a spare which meant that I got a free phone call now and then. Of course, we had to be very careful what we said as you knew damn well that the other girls would be listening in on your conversation. There was only room for one single man in the Detachment office building so when we had two single men, I made the High Prairie Hotel my home.

There was very little major crime anywhere in the Peace River country. Break and entries, minor thefts and the odd assault took up a lot of our time. We would get the odd drunk driver, but that was still a hard offence to prove as there were no breathalysers and the driver had to be falling down drunk before you had a sure case. Drunks were common but we took as many homes as we charged. Suicides were as much of a sad problem then as they are population wise now. I remember a couple that stand out, not because of the suicide itself but for the activities that followed. One was at Slave Lake where a guy had hung himself in the bush in the middle of winter. When we got there, you might say he was "a stretched out stiff." There was no such thing as EMS or body movers so after a lot of pushing and shoving we finally got him propped up cornerwise in the back seat of our car. When we got back to the detachment the garage was heated with an oil stove and we couldn't leave him there to thaw out, making the outhouse the only other place. So we propped him up in the corner of that building where he spent the night. Next morning Cst. Norm Goodfellow was the first to answer the call of nature, and Gordon and I had "inadvertently" forgotten to tell him the building was already occupied but we were standing at the window waiting for the results. Well – Norm came flying out with his breeks and long john's around his ankles, his braces flapping in the breeze and his steps were about ten feet apart. He flew through the door shouting "There's a, there's a", by that time we were laughing so hard we could hardly stand up and he soon realized that he had been had. He failed to see any bright side in our black humour, and I think that was one of his reasons for requesting an office job - with inside plumbing.

The other suicide that stands out was at High Prairie when a Ukrainian farmer out by Grouard hung himself in his own barn. With no phone service the message was relayed to us through several different people. Cpl. Harry Beggs and I answered the call and sure enough we found him hanging from a rafter in the loft of his barn. About the time we got him to cut down his wife, who was great with child, decided that she was going into labour – now. A young son, about ten or so, was running around screaming in a state of panic and stepped on a very sharp axe, cutting deeply into the arch of his foot. We stuffed dad into the trunk, put mother in the back seat and told her she was not having the baby in our car if we had to tie her legs together, and put the kid in the front seat between us. With Harry driving we headed for the High Prairie Hospital. I started wrapping the kid's foot with roller bandages from our emergency kit, but no matter how many wraps I put on it kept bleeding. It was time for a tourniquet, but I had nothing to turn it with so hauled out my revolver and I guess the kid thought I was going to shoot him as he really started to holler. I put three or four loose wraps around his ankle, stuck the barrel of my gun through it and twisted it up tight enough to stop the bleeding. We made record time to the hospital, dropped mum and the kid off in front, recovered my revolver, took dad around back to the cooler for later examination by the Coroner. Another routine patrol and Harry casually suggests, "You know I think it's time for a coffee."

With no EMS or ambulances, the Police were often first responders and we had compulsory Red Cross training sessions every year in conjunction with the annual revolver shoot. The forests throughout the Peace River were filled with small, mostly private sawmills during the winter months. Every winter a man somewhere had a disagreement with the big circular saw and ended up dead or badly injured. We had one of those accidents south of High Prairie and Dr. Charles Woods and I responded with him driving. He always had the biggest Chrysler car in town and drove like a madman. We found the injured man in the cook shack, which had one small window and the open door. Dr. Woods did a quick examination and decided, "We can't move him like this, I'll have to sew him up – clean off the table." Up to that time the door had been full of faces, but it instantly emptied out and we were on our own. We cleaned off the table, lifted him up and started cutting off his clothes. No scrubs here, I administered the chloroform under the surgeon's directions, and he hauled together the torn up body parts and started rough stitching them together. When we had him stabilized, we loaded him into the car and headed back to the hospital where he underwent more surgery. To my surprise the guy lived, although I don't think he ever went back to work. He was certainly not the only person I helped sew up, but he was the most serious. Police work in the north was a multi-tasking occupation, but it was never dull.

Something else that took up a lot of our time and had nothing to do with police work were sudden deaths and estates. There were a lot of old bachelors living alone in remote locations. They usually died in winter and would be found by some neighbour who noticed that there was no smoke coming from their shacks for several days in a row. Such a typical death occurred just south of Valleyview when I was policing that area. This guy lived quite a ways off the main road and there was only a sleigh track into his house. He attended the New Year's Eve dance, caught a ride to his gate and started walking to his house with a case of beer under his arm. He got to within 100 feet from his house, had a heart attack and fell dead. When we got to him, he was frozen solid, lying in the sleigh track with his hat pushed back and the case of beer still tucked under his arm. Death was obviously instantaneous. Our first problem was getting him into High Prairie so that the Coroner could verify the cause of death. A local farmer with a team and sleigh helped us haul him out to the road, but he wouldn't fit in our car. There was logging going on south along the new #34 highway and we knew that sooner or later a truck load of logs would come along heading for High Prairie. We rolled him in a tarp, tied him on top of the load of logs and that solved our problem. A few eyebrows were raised when they saw a load of logs going through town with a stiff tied on top holding them down.

We had to go back to his house numerous times looking for anything that might hold a clue as to his next of kin. There was nothing, not a will, not a letter not a scrap of paper anywhere to indicate possible relatives or even where he may have come from. All the neighbours knew was that he came up from the United States many years ago and was the local bootlegger. We didn't find a still but come spring we had no trouble "sniffing" out his hiding place which was in the rafter space between the first and second floors and was accessed through loose boards under his bed. There were still corks and empty bottles lying around, so some of his product must have still been working when he bottled it. The smell was still in the wood and there was no doubt that he had been making home brew. Fortunately, his only livestock was a couple of horses and a neighbour undertook looking after them. We had to secure the house and keep checking it periodically. The months kept passing and with no next of kin being found the Alberta Government finally approved the sale of land and property. Oh joy – now we had to list everything and organize an auction sale. We managed to get the sale in before it snowed, and after the auctioneer and all the other bills were paid, we forwarded everything to Edmonton for the Government coffers. We eventually heard that a next of kin had been found but, in the meantime, we had spent days and days on something that had nothing whatsoever to do with police work. Our duties were often neither exciting nor rewarding but our presence and dedication was always appreciated.

Helen only taught the one year in Peace River 1949/50. She then took a business course at McTavish Business College in Edmonton. On completion of that course she returned to Peace River and got a job in accounting at Horne and Pitfield. They were the biggest wholesale produce distributors in the area and although her work was demanding, she enjoyed having set hours and weekends off. She could catch the bus down to High Prairie on Friday night and back to Peace River on Sunday. As I mentioned, you had to have cash and assets of $1,200.00 before you could get married. I had the full amount by June 1st, 1952 and submitted the necessary paperwork. It was our plan to get married in September shortly after my 24th birthday. All my requests were through the O.C. Peace River Sub/Division and had to go all the way up to the Commr. for final approval. Copies of some of the bureaucratic and childish nonsense are shown below. You will note in the one dated July 17, 1952 that Helen's name has been erased before it could be sent to me even though her passing had been well reported to Ottawa. I guess it just goes to show that the extent of Government bureaucratic stupidity has not changed much in sixty years.

In late July 1952 I got word that I was to be transferred to Grande Prairie Detachment. This is what I wanted for if I was to stay in the Peace River country it would have to be either Grande Prairie or Peace River. Fortunately, Helen and I had been planning ahead and I was aware of a young female Native on the Driftpile Reserve with TB. She had refused all efforts to go voluntarily to the sanatorium in Edmonton. We arranged for her forceful evacuation on a Friday, Helen was to be the matron and we would take her to Edmonton in my car. I got mileage and Helen got paid. Money was tight and we were saving all we could for our honeymoon. We bought a bed, chesterfield and a kitchen suite at a wholesale outlet and arranged for them to be sent to Grande Prairie at a later date. I found a little one-bedroom bungalow for us to rent from Jack and Lois Lyle and had our furniture shipped from Edmonton. Our furnishings were rather sparse, but I had the place liveable by the time we got married.

Re: Reg. # 15336 - Cst. A.G. Elliott
Application for Permission to Marry.

O.C. "K" DIVISION,
R.C.M. POLICE,
EDMONTON, ALTA.   400/26 JUL 14 52

1.   Forwarded and recommended.

2.   Should this application be approved, I
intend to transfer Constable Elliott before the marriage
is solemnized. At the present time I have in mind
transferring him to Grande Prairie for duty at that
point. The principal reason for effecting his transfer
is due to the fact that single men's quarters are
available at High Prairie and I consider it advisable
to have one single man at that point for obvious
reasons.

                                   [signature] Inspr.
                                   K. Shakespeare.
Peace River, Alta.   Comdg. Peace River S/Divn.
8-7-52.

The Commissioner
R.C.M. Police
Ottawa, Ontario

1.   Forwarded for your information. The above named
Cst. has enumerated his assets which appear to be adequate.
He is twenty-four years of age and has a mature outlook on
life and I consider, realizes his responsibilities fully.
Application is recommended for consideration.

                                   [signature]
Edmonton   (H. P. Mathewson, Supt.)
10-7-52   for O. C. "K" Division, A.O.L.

              APPROVED   Not before
              [signature]   9-9-52
              Asst. Comm'r

S.F. 15336
                                   July 17, 1952

MEMORANDUM to:

The O.C. "K" Div.,
R.C.M.P., Edmonton.

              Re: 15336, Constable Elliott, A. G.

              Referring to your minute of the 10th instant,
the application of the above named for permission to marry
                                   has been
approved, but the marriage is not to be solemnized before
9-9-52, when Constable Elliott will have reached the age of
24 years.

2.   Please have Constable Elliott report in due course
when the ceremony has been performed, at the same time
forwarding his wife's birth certificate and their marriage
certificate for photostating.

GHP/B   (G.H. Prime), Insp.,
                                   Asst. Adjutant.

Grande Prairie

I was officially transferred to Grande Prairie on September 1st, 1952. It was cheaper to transfer a single man than wait until I was married. The Non-Commissioned Officer I/C. Grande Prairie Detachment was Sgt. Sid Murray. He was not the nicest man to work for nor was he that well-liked by the members. He was also not well known nor particularly well liked in the town. They were not overly social and did not partake in many of the public activities. Their living quarters were part of the office building, his wife was a bit of a witch and cleanliness was not her forte. There was frequently a foot or two of empty tin cans left in their back porch to be cleaned out periodically by the Detachment Csts. I know what a pig's pen her house was as I made numerous trips through it every fall and spring. I got stuck with getting the storm windows out of the basement and putting them up and taking them down for two years in a row. The building was two stories and I had to use a ladder. I'm sure my fingerprints were on some of the window frames until the building was demolished. Those old wood windows were heavy and I knew I'd be fired if I ever dropped one.

Helen and I were married on September 20th, 1952 and made the second big RCMP Red Serge wedding of the year as Jeanie and David were married in May. Jeanie was Helen's matron of honour and Cst. Gordon Stratton was my best man. The ushers were Cpl. Doug Banting and Cst. McKinstry. My second usher was to be Cst. Don Kirk from High Prairie but he got tied up with work and couldn't make it so Cst. McKinstry was pressed into service at the last minute. Helen's dad was also in

Red Serge and even the O.C. got into formal uniform for the occasion. Helen was a very popular young lady in Peace River and since the service was open the church was filled to overflowing. I was largely unknown and was "The guy that Helen married." The double ring ceremony was performed in a setting of white gladioli (Helen's favourite flower) while the church was decorated with sweet peas, ferns and fall leaves. Mum and Dad drove up for the wedding and arrived in Peace River a couple of days in advance.

There were a lot of tricks played by members on the young guys getting married and I had been involved in more than a couple.

Helen and I on our wedding day

I didn't expect to escape without some skullduggery so had been dropping accidental hints about Edmonton as our destination following the wedding and leaving early. After the ceremonies were all over and the party was well underway, we sneaked off and headed for Grande Prairie. There were two routes up the south hill out of Peace River and when Gordon Stratton found that we had left, he and several other members jumped into a car and raced up the hill to overtake us and "kidnap" Helen. As it happened a car similar to mine was coming up the hill and I can only imagine the look on that poor bugger's face when three half snapped Red Serge Mounties jumped out and pulled him over. By the time they got back to the party we had escaped. I had secretly told Mum what our plans were so that she and Dad could join us the next day and see our little rental house in Grande Prairie.

In early January 1953 I was sent to Fairmount Training Centre in Vancouver for a six-week refresher course. This left Helen alone which was not a happy situation after being married for only three months. Helen was working for the city by then and accepted my absence as part of being a "Mountie's wife." I didn't

Dad, Mom and I

know it at the time, but records show I was second out of 30 with a 90% average. Helen always wanted to have her own house, and this was on her list long before we got married. In the spring of 1953, we decided that if we were ever going to get our own house, we had to start some time and the sooner the better. With this in mind we decided to sell our car and walk, Helen would work for one year and we'd build a home in Grande Prairie. We found plans for a 1024-foot bungalow, giving us two bedrooms, kitchen with dinette and living room. I took the contract myself and secured a CMHC mortgage at 6% over 25 years. Everyone from the Sgt. on down thought we were absolutely crazy and were not hesitant in telling us so. Their reasoning was that we would be moved in three years, would be broke and stuck with a house we could neither sell nor afford. Most of it was mere jealousy. I had the help and advice of a nice old professional home builder called Jack Horne and over the course of about six months I built our first home. It was mostly all hand work and Jack helped me with his crew when extra manpower was needed. His only instructions to me were that it had to be built right and it had to be square. It was.

Another nice thing about it was that we built right next door to Jack and Lois Lyle whose cottage we were renting. Jack was a travelling salesman for GWG (Great West Garment Co). They made blue jeans in an Edmonton factory and when a new seamstress was learning to sew, she practised on jeans for dolls and little kids. Eventually, my two eldest boys, Danny and David, had jeans that no other kid in Grande Prairie could find or buy and best of all they were free. I also had the use of Jack's car when he was not away traveling. They had three girls a little older than our boys, so we got to be babysitters for them in payment for the free use of their car.

As soon as I got to Grande Prairie, I became involved with the Boy Scout movement and before I knew it I was the Scout Master. I was also involved in the scouting movement in Slave Lake, but it was not as organized as in Grande Prairie where I had lots of community support. I had never been a scout myself, so a lot of my training was made up as I went. One thing I was very familiar with was First Aid as I had taken many courses by then. I passed this along and it helped save a life. The road south of Grande Prairie was gravel and very dusty. There were a lot of gravel trucks on it and one evening the Scout troop was out on an unsupervised hike when they happened to be at the right place at the right time. With no air conditioning in cars, the habit was to roll down the windows and drive with your elbow sticking out in the fresh air. A gravel truck and a car collided and tore the car driver's arm off at the elbow. The Scouts sprang into action, made a tourniquet out of their scarves, bound the guy up and sent him off to hospital, saving his life. When the dust had cleared, they found his severed arm and brought it into the detachment office. I was not in the office but the member on duty rushed the arm over to the hospital. Unfortunately, re-attachment was impossible.

My Scouts got a nice write up in the local paper but that is about all. When I got down to civilization in the Calgary area and saw what Scouts were getting Governor Generals commendations for, I regretted that no one in Grande Prairie thought to seek rewards for "My Heroes." I was at a Scout Troop meeting and walking home to our new house on February 19th, 1954 when from about two blocks away I heard Helen pounding hell out of our piano with "In The Mood." I picked up the pace and was running by the time I got home. Helen had gone into labor; Danny was on his way and she was in no mood for – those damn scouts. I rushed her off to the hospital and by morning we were Proud Parents. I continued on with the Scouts but with added police duties and being a parent, I scaled back my activities and camping trips.

I was involved in my first murder trial in Grande Prairie. It wasn't much of an investigation just two men in an argument gone badly and one of them got killed. With just over six years of service I became the senior investigator. With any major crime you have to make meticulous notes on every step of your investigation so that they can be referred to in court. My notes were limited at the best, were not made at the scene and I was denied referral to them at the time of trial. We got a conviction on a lesser charge, which was appropriate, but I would certainly have profited by some timely advice from a good supervisor. I got my lessons the hard way and never forgot my first real courtroom grilling.

I had another interesting case in Grande Prairie which involved a bunch of petty thefts. Minor thefts had been going on for a year or so and we knew it had to be someone local but had no suspects. I then got a tip from the public that it was the Post Master's son. No one ever suspected him and the Post Master was a respected stalwart of the community. After a few minutes of questioning the guy fessed up and started revealing crimes that were still unreported. We started with a couple of search warrants and then the whole thing started spiraling out of control. We were recovering property faster than we could keep track of the individual items. There was a MacLeod's Hardware Store on the main street with a back-door right across the alley from the Post Office. The Post Office was a new two-story Federal building with residences on the top floor. Our suspect (after sixty years I don't remember his name) would walk through the hardware, pick up a box of tools and casually walk out the back door. We ended up with at least a dozen tool boxes, plus numerous new items, all with the MacLeod label still on them. The store first denied the thefts until we showed them the pile of recoveries then they went into shock. We also recovered a stolen vehicle hidden in the bush and a boat, motor and trailer buried in a farmer's straw stack. These items required a tow truck to recover them and soon not only was the office full of exhibits, but the driveway was filling up. Our office was filling up and Sgt. Murray had to find secure storage space. The only Federal building in town was the Post Office. So, our neat piles of exhibits were moved before we ever got them properly recorded on exhibits reports. That took almost a week, our case was a mess and the accused had access to our exhibits. Fortunately, he pled guilty to a litany of charges and we spent the next year trying to find owners for all our exhibits. With my lifetime of wisdom and experience with the culprit, I deduced the kid was gay, unfortunately had no friends and was stealing just for the thrill of it. There was no evidence that he ever used or sold any of the stolen items.

It was in the summer of 1956 in Grande Prairie that I got my one and only "Black mark" in my entire RCMP Service. I'm ashamed of it and wish it had never happened, but if I am to record my history, I must tell the bad as well as the good. My Sgt., Syd Murray, was away on holiday, one car was in the garage for repairs, I had been working my butt off and we had two young boys at home to look after. I was working late on a case when the Sgt. called from Valleyview to say his car broke down and I was to send someone out with the one remaining police car and a rope to tow him home. I wouldn't go to get him but dispatched a recruit to tow him home. As I was still working on a case, I walked over to the Town Office to see if I could borrow their car for half an hour. Cst. Haubrick was sitting in the office and didn't need the car at that moment but he got a smirk on his face and said,

"No it's a town car and you can't have it." After the fight with the Sgt. and walking over in the rain I had had it and without even thinking I popped the SOB in the nose.

He started to whimper like a baby and promptly drove himself up to the hospital, making the matter public. Cst. Kal Mains. I/C Town Detail told the Sgt. who called the O.C. and Cst. Elliott was headed for the Orderly Room charged with "Disgraceful Conduct." A couple of weeks later I had to go over to Peace River and appear before the O.C. I had to be in Red Serge (but no spurs) and was escorted by a Non-Commissioned Officer into a trial before the O.C.. I admitted my transgressions, apologized for my conduct and then explained what led up to the incident. I had no objections to rescuing the Sgt. and his wife if their car broke down, but I didn't think that under the circumstances our one remaining police vehicle should be used as a tow truck. I was fined $35.00 plus $1.50 for Cst. Haubrick's medical bill. An appeal for clemency was written to the Commr. on my behalf by Cpl. Banting (the usher at my wedding) which resulted in the fine being reduced to $20.00 and the medical bill forgiven. Within about three months Sgt. Murray was transferred out and replaced by Sgt. Percy Keys. The Detachment took on a new and more pleasant atmosphere, which lead to guys questioning why I hadn't done something stupid a whole lot sooner.

Having an orderly charge on your record is not a good thing, but it didn't affect me to any great extent. I still received my Good Conduct medal and ribbon after 20 years of service and my discharge certificate shows my service as being EXEMPLARY. The best you can get. One of my neighbours and good friends in Grande Prairie had a farm. I helped him thrash that fall and made up the $20.00 so that we could still pay our bills. We hadn't replaced our car as yet. With house payments and with Helen not working money was tight.

My most lasting reward for my five years in Grande Prairie was joining the Masonic Lodge. It all started by a visit to Grande Prairie by Ned Rivers and Dave Little. Rivers was a former member of the APP (Alberta Provincial Police) and a retiree from the RCMP. They were making a tour of the Peace River country and stopped for a visit with Sgt. Keys. I was assigned to help them with farm access for goose hunting around Saskatoon Lake. Masonry came up and I professed I didn't know much about it other than that they had a good reputation and seemed to be leaders in the community. Before long I was approached by a mechanic from the Ford dealership and presented with an application to join Grande Prairie Lodge No.

105 GRA. (Grand Registry of Alberta). I found out later that Ned Rivers was Secretary of The Grand Lodge of Alberta and Dave Little was a Masonic Past Grand Master. I reconnected with Ned Rivers when I came to Cochrane and he became my best friend and Masonic mentor. As well as being secretary for the Alberta Masonic Lodge, Ned was also secretary for the RCMP Veterans Association for all of Canada. I received my First Degree in Masonry on July 12th, 1956 and my Master Masons' Degree on March 30th, 1957. I was only able to attend two Lodge meetings before being transferred to Fort Vermillion.

In the early spring of 1957, Father (Helen's dad) broke the news to us that the O.C. was considering transferring me to Fort Vermilion. This was not welcome news as it was only a Constable's Detachment. The living quarters were terrible, and we were hoping to move south, not north. On June 17 we got the formal letter that I was heading for the bush. The O.C. told Father that he knew he could send me to Fort Vermillion, "As all Curly needed is a ham sandwich and an axe." In the three years that followed with all its trials, tribulations and challenges I began to fully understand the meaning of his comment. Helen and I discussed our options but, in the Force, there were really no options, you did as you were told or got a new job. That outlook was not for either one of us, so we accepted the transfer. We knew it would only be for three years as they never let the policeman's kids go to the public school. The Natives would beat them up the first day.

We sold our house privately for a little over $14,000. This put around $1,400.00 in our bank account, or three years wages for me. Helen was adamant that we were keeping this for our future home, and it would not be touched under any circumstances - which we did. We took summer holidays to visit Jeanie and Dave in British Columbia. We returned via Calgary as I wanted to show Helen the detachment building at East Coulee in the Drumheller area. This was reported to be the absolute worst RCMP building in Canada. When I found what the accommodation was like in Fort Vermilion, I don't think East Coulee should have been rated number one. While we were in British Columbia we bought a little golden lab puppy dog, "Chico", as a pet for the boys and a guard dog for Helen. He ended up weighing about 90 pounds and exceeded all of our expectations for a family pet.

My Three Years at Fort Vermilion

The moving truck packed up all our meagre belongings in Grand Prairie on August 13, Helen's favourite number. We stayed one night with Helen's folks in Peace River and the next day headed for Fort Vermilion. The moving truck was stuck three times between High Level and Fort Vermilion, and I wondered if we would have any furniture left at all by the time we arrived. Of course, it was raining, and the movers took one day to unpack our stuff and another to load up Vern Smith's furniture, who I was replacing. I officially took over my first detachment on August 15th, 1957. It was disappointing and yet in some ways exciting.

The Detachment building had been the former summerhouse of "Twelve-Foot Davis" who had died in 1902. Henry F. Davis was prospecting in the Cariboo Gold Rush in British Columbia when he found that two lucrative and adjacent claims were 12 feet larger than allowed. He filed a claim on this narrow piece of land and extracted $30,000 worth of gold. A fortune at that time, and thus was forever known as "Twelve-Foot Davis." He came to the Peace River country and established a network of trading posts in direct competition to the Hudson's Bay Company (HBC). His headquarters were at Fort Vermillion and his summerhouse became the RCMP detachment until I closed it down in 1959.

The main building was two stories, with the bottom built of logs and covered with shiplap and the top story of rough lumber. The building faced west towards the river with a lean-to all down the north side, which was the office, cell room and the storeroom. Across the back was another lean-to, which housed the kitchen and another storeroom. The original log portion was divided into three rooms each being 15 x 19 feet. The kitchen had the same dimensions. There were three bedrooms upstairs. Keeping the place warm took five stoves, three oil heaters, a propane cook stove which we brought with us, and a six-hole wood burning kitchen range which came from the O.C.'s house in Peace River. The latter was a godsend to our existence and saved the day on more than one occasion. There was no running water except for on the floor of the storeroom next to the kitchen where we had a 45-gallon fuel barrel for a water container with a pipe going through the outside wall to a funnel. Jack Whitehouse was the water man who would bring us water once or twice a week. He had the same size barrel as ours, but invariably he would run ours over onto the floor. This was no problem in the summertime but in the wintertime, it created a solid block of ice on the floor. In the wintertime there was not enough heat in the building to keep this water barrel from freezing over every night. In the cold Jack would just walk in through the back, across the kitchen floor, lift the lid off the wood stove and warm his hands. We could never convince him to knock and his theory was that "You knew I was here I just filled up your barrel." He was just one of the colourful characters that we came to accept.

There were a couple of more surprises that I had not been warned about. Firstly, we had electricity in the house, but it was largely in name only. A local businessman, Billie Batt, had set up a power plant and over the years had run a power line down the Main Street. The RCMP detachment was near the end of the line. There were no transformers on the line and our lights flickered in time with the firing of the diesel engine. This was alright in the daytime but when it got dark and people started turning on their lights we had to run and unplug our deep-freeze. Instead of getting 120 volts we were down to as low as 65. Fortunately, in the wintertime it was seldom necessary to plug our deepfreeze in as the inside storage room temperature was cold enough to keep things frozen.

With no running water the toilet was a closet in the upstairs sleeping area equipped with a five-gallon oil can for a honey bucket. Helen and I had experienced outdoor plumbing growing up so we could manage, but it was a bit of an adventure convincing two little boys that this was their inside potty. I made sure the bucket didn't get too full as I had to carry it down a flight of stairs to the outhouse. It was always the last thing I did for Helen before I went on any trips. Exciting eh!!

Fort Vermilion was my first posting as Detachment Commander. I was all alone. There were no communications with Sub/Division Head Quarters and my nearest back-up was 125 miles away, but they may as well have been on the moon. By the first Christmas I knew and had established good working relations with most of the settlers in the community. The Natives had their own little area known as "Chicago Town." They were friendly enough but did not partake in any of the civic activities. Without interactions with them it was hard to build confidence and I knew some of my predecessors had not treated them with much respect. There were always a few around looking for trouble and that came to a head in spades on New Year's Eve.

The village hall where everything took place was only a block from the office. I still had no Force vehicle so around 11:00 o'clock I put on my police parka and wandered over to the hall to see what was going on. As soon as I got through the door, I saw one of the village troublemakers acting up and he had obviously been drinking. I walked over to him only intending to tell him to calm down and behave himself. Before I knew what was happening, I had a fight on my hands. I then tried to affect an arrest and drag him out of the hall. All was going well until we reached the door and then three of his friends jumped me. I was on the ground; they were putting the boots to me big time and one of the four was trying to gouge my right eye out. Eye gouging was a common practice among the Natives. Fortunately, three or four community members came in to rescue me, but by then I was pretty beat up and my eye was bleeding. All four of the combatants escaped but I knew the original one as Gaston Cardinal as he was a known troublemaker. I could not identify the other three for court purposes, but it did not take me long to find out their names.

I had Dr. Doug Cassidy check my eye but all he could do was put some ointment on it. I was damn mad, and my eye hurt so the best thing I could have done was go to bed and wait for the New Year. However, if I had done that, every tough guy in town would have been ready for a fight every time I made an arrest. So – I got into full uniform, including a loaded side arm, tracked Cardinal down, arrested him for assault and locked him up for the night. The result was that I had a loud drunk locked up on New Year's Eve and the cell right next to the kitchen. I charged him with assaulting a Peace Officer and the local Magistrate released him on bail. He pled not guilty on the grounds that I was not in uniform and he didn't know I was a Policeman. S/Sgt. Allan from Peace River came up and conducted the trial. The Magistrate did not buy into his not knowing me and sentenced him to a few months in jail.

It didn't take too long for my eye to heal up and I thought I had survived with no permanent injuries. I found that not to be true when hunting season came in the fall and I could not focus with my right eye. There were no optometrists in the Peace River country, and it was over a year before I had the injury properly checked in Edmonton. X-rays revealed that I had scar tissue on the back of my retina. This was not repairable and there has never been technology invented to fix the problem. It was not until after I came to Calgary that a disability board was convened on this work-related injury and I was granted a disability pension. This pension is about $500 per month, tax-free and was reduced when the boys reached 21. This has added up over the past 50 years, but I would much, much, rather have had the site in the eye.

When we arrived in Fort Vermilion, I saw that the Police Jeep had several flat tires and looked like it was past due for the garbage dump. I found out that it had not been running for months and that my predecessor Cst. Vern Smith had made little effort to have it replaced as he knew that he was being moved. There was not one car dealership in my whole detachment area, and it was necessary to have the wreck hauled out to Peace River before any bids for a replacement vehicle could be obtained. It was the spring of 1958 before I got a new vehicle. A Chevrolet six-cylinder panel truck with four-wheel-drive and winch installed by Bluebird Auto in Lethbridge replaced the old jeep. Unfortunately, this came with tubeless tires which were totally useless. Any frozen rut would break the seal on the tire and when I put chains on it cracked the weld between the rim and the wheel. It took another six months for me to get a set of 16-inch truck rims and tires. Until I got the new police vehicle, I used my own car on a mileage basis for the good roads, which weren't many, and rented vehicles for the bushwhacking trips.

The only thing that appeared anywhere near new and worked as it should was the police canoe. This was a 20-foot Peterborough Great Lake Freighter with an 18 horsepower Evinrude outboard motor. The motor was a little short on horsepower, but the canoe was very stable and perfect for a big river. We kept the canoe on land until the spring flood was over and then I chained it to a tree on the riverbank across the road from the office. I had enough gas cans for 50 gallons of gas, which is about what I needed for the trip up the river or downriver to the end of my detachment area.

Speaking of the detachment area, I had a big chunk of the northwest corner of Alberta. There was only one main gravelled highway through the area which is #35 and it ran from Peace River to the Northwest Territories border. I covered everything north of Keg River, which was a distance of 280 Kms. My area went from the British Columbian border on the west to the fifth Meridian on the east. My farthest down river trip was to a Hudson's Bay Company post at the 5th, meridian. The HBC building was right on the river and has been since washed away and the area is now called Garden River. The whole area covered about 35,000 square miles with a total population of maybe 3,000 people. The only all-weather roads were #35 highway and #58 from High Level to Fort Vermillion. The road from Fort Vermillion south to the Mennonite area of La Crete and Buffalo Head Prairie had some gravel but was mostly a dirt road.

We had no telephone and there was no communication with headquarters at Peace River except by telegraph. This was most unreliable as the line was old and not being repaired. If it was working the calligrapher was frequently away trapping or deep into the sauce. The Alberta Forestry Service and the HBC had their own radio communications, but these were also unreliable as they went through repeater stations. My best communication was by mail as we had a daily bus service which operated year-round except for the spring and fall break up when the ferry was not operating. During these times the mail was sometimes taken by some hardy soul in a canoe from the north side of the river to ice solid enough to walk on, pulled across the ice to the south side on a toboggan, then changed back to a second canoe to reach the south bank. The hundred feet or so along the riverbanks were always the last to freeze over and the first to thaw in the spring.

With no police vehicle, I didn't do much traveling during the first eight months which took me over to the spring of 1958. I spent a lot of time in the office reading operational manuals and made sure I kept the office returns in shape and timely. It was also a good time to make friends and establish my presence in the village. There was no municipal representation, council or any sort of civil oversight in the village. I soon found out that ninety percent of my work was not police, but social services. Because of the remoteness and lack of communications I also had a number of special appointments. The most prestigious one was an appointment from the Federal Privy Council in Ottawa as a Judge of The Federal Court for the purposes of the Citizenship Act. This was a wonderful big flowery document which I had to surrender as soon as I was "posted outside." I did use it once – but more on that later. The second was a certificate as a Marriage Commr. for the Province of Alberta. I didn't get to perform any marriages, but I did talk a couple out of it - which was just as good at the time. They were young, of mixed religions and were afraid of their parent's reactions. The other two were writs under the Liquor and Customs and Excise Acts. This meant I made searches under "reasonable beliefs" and did not have to wait days or travel hundreds of miles to get a judicial warrant.

There were three schools in the village, a public school, Roman Catholic public school and a four room Indian residential school. The residential school was by far the biggest building in the village as it not only housed the four school rooms, but also the hospital and was home for the nuns and staff. The head priest, or father and all the brothers had a separate building. All the buildings were heated by wood and they went through massive piles of cordwood over the winter. There was one doctor, a Roman Catholic Irishman by the name of Doug Cassidy. He was a bit of a character with two girls the same age as our boys and we became good friends.

There was a small Anglican church which soon became our Sunday home. The priest was a young single fellow called Gavin Barnett. He was from the Montreal area and soon became one of our family. We later stayed with him when we went to Montreal for Expo 67. The second biggest employer at the Fort was the Federal Experimental farm. The superintendent was Hank Anderson. He and his wife Margaret had five kids, two girls and three boys. Karol was the oldest and she now lives in the condos at Bears Paw. Don and family are in Calgary, Bruce in Regina, Chris and John are both musicians in Toronto. The experimental farm had their own electricity, lighting and running water so we were rather envious of them. We had them down to the barracks for our second Christmas and were feeling rather bad for our antiquated accommodation. However, when they arrived, they burst through the back door and ran for the big kitchen wood stove. Their water pipes had frozen and they had no heat whatsoever. Sometimes newer is not necessarily better.

Our other good friends were Jack and Pearl Newman. Jack had a farm just out of town and he also worked part-time for the Indian department. They had a son Gerry who was the same age as Danny, and they played together quite often. Jack and I made many trips together with the Indian agencies' bombardier. Shortly after we arrived in Fort Vermilion Ted and Betty Giles arrived with their family. Ted was the school district superintendent and looked after schools in about the same area I had. They were also Anglicans; we'd known them in Peace River, and they were a nice addition to our circle of friends.

With the small population of Fort Vermilion, I pretty well knew everyone in town after the first winter. Of course, not all were friends but there are two more that I must include. The first is Wayne and Evelyn Wright. Wayne was an American flying farmer with his main base at Wellton Arizona. He had two Canadian operations, one at Fort Vermillion and another at Wawanesa, Manitoba. He chose these locations for the soil content and remoteness from all others seeds to prevent contamination. He dealt only in registered grass seeds. His Fort Vermilion Farm consisted of several thousand acres totally removed from any other farming area and was about 12 miles upriver from the village. It was only accessible by air or a winding dirt road through the bush. They also owned the original Hudson's Bay property located at the downriver end of the village. The Factor's house was the only building still in existence and it went back to the mid-1800s. Wayne had built a large heated storage shed on the property as everything coming in for the farm was dropped off in the village. They spent their winters in Arizona and had a full-time farm manager who lived on the farm with his wife.

Wayne started off with a Cessna 172, and graduated to a Cessna Cardinal and ended up with a Cessna 182. None of these planes flew more than about 125 mph and it usually took him two days to fly from Wellton to Fort Vermilion. In the summer his was often the only wheeled aircraft at the local airport and he was always available whenever I had to cross the river in the spring or fall break up. He was also never reluctant to make a mercy flight when one was necessary. It was his aircraft and under his tutelage that I got my first flying lessons.

The next person I have to include is, after Helen, the best unpaid "second man" I ever had. His name is Narcisse Lizotte, a Metis, who had been the Force guide and interpreter for years. He was about 65 years of age when I arrived on the scene and became not only a guide but a companion and mentor. He came from a family of 16, eight boys and eight girls, all of whom lived to a hundred except two, a boy and a girl, who died in the 1918 flu epidemic. I don't know what education Narcisse had, if any, but his knowledge was all on his surroundings and the people of that area. He could tell tribe, family and exactly where they were from just by the beadwork on their moccasins. Every mark, every track, every movement of birds, clouds or water meant something to him, and he was always ready to explain it. He not only spoke the language, but he knew most of the Natives in the area - the good, bad and in between. He was the Jerry Potts of my 26-year RCMP career. I never went down river without him unless it was Treaty paying time and then we had a flotilla of riverboats and he was not needed.

There were three Treaty paying points in the Detachment areas - Fort Vermilion, Habay (now Rainbow Lake) and Little Red River/Fox Lake. There were several small reserves between High Level and Fort Vermilion, but the Indians would always make it into "The Fort" for their money. Fort Vermilion was the economic centre of the area and most of the money was spent before they went back to their reserves. Habay was a fly in destination and the routine was similar to the treaties I paid as a young Cst. The more interesting and complicated was the trip down river as it involved a portage both ways around the Fort Vermilion Chutes – a stretch of un-navigable river about four miles in length. There was no electricity in that area which meant taking your own power plant and gasoline to run the x-ray equipment. All adults and any teenager suspected of having TB were x-rayed before they got their treaty payment. The TB test results would come back in the late fall or winter and often lead to me enforcing a compulsory evacuation to the TB sanatorium in Edmonton. Not my favourite *Police work*.

The treaty flotilla involved at least three boats: 1) A light canoe for the Indian Agent and one or two passengers; 2) the Police canoe loaded with passengers and often bulky stuff like bundles of blankets; 3) and then one or two slow flat-bottomed boats with everything from the x-ray power plant to farm machinery. The Force was too cheap to provide life jackets, but I had my own which was a used RCAF WWII surplus one from the army surplus store. (I still have it amongst the useless treasures in our storeroom). I had to be in Red Serge to pay treaty or the Indians wouldn't take the money, so I travelled in boots and breeches - a sure way to drown if you ever capsized or went overboard. The Indian Department personnel usually consisted of a doctor, dentist and at least one x-ray technician. Then there were always at least a couple of Ottawa bureaucrats whose only reason to exist seemed to be to enjoy a free holiday and maybe a canoe trip down the Mighty Peace. They certainly never helped with any of the manual labour involved or added anything for the good of the Natives. The barges never went beyond rapids, but the Police freight canoe could carry 5000 lbs and was always the one that got to be portaged. We had a reliable native with a team and wagon and he would back into the river, load the canoe, haul it the four miles downriver on dirt track and dump it back in below the rapids. I paid him $5.00 for the round trip and collected it on my expense account. The Roman Catholic Fox Lake Settlement was a good mile from the river, there was no dock, so you just tied your boat to a tree and hiked the rest of the way.

During my three years at the Fort I made many canoe trips down river for work and pleasure, all were routine, and I never encountered any adventures or mishaps. One time I was alone and was just out for a boat ride when I came upon a young black bear swimming across the river, which was over a kilometre wide at that point. I started harassing him and was having lots of fun seeing how close I could get when the little bugger decided he could also play around and decided to come on board. As I was just out for a joy ride, I had no gun with me and had to dispatch him with a canoe paddle as he was not about to disembark on his own. I survived but the bear and the paddle did not. I had to make up quite a cock and bull story to get the paddle replaced. I brought the bear home where Danny and David got their picture taken with it before I gave it to an Indian.

Down river with a light load - 3 hours

8 men and 1000s of pounds in pouring rain

I only made one lengthy trip upriver and that was with Ted Giles, the School Superintendent and a young Cst. from Manning Detachment. We went all the way up to Carcajou, which was the border between our two Detachment areas. The only buildings at Carcajou were a post office and a small trading post. There were no roads into it and even in I only made one lengthy trip upriver and that was with Ted Giles, the School Superintendent and a young Cst. from Manning Detachment. We went all the way up to Carcajou, which was the border between our two Detachment areas. The only buildings at Carcajou were a post office and a small trading post. There were no roads into it and even in winter it was difficult to access. The trip was over 100 miles upriver and I had to lay up a cache of gas in the Buffalo Head Prairie district as this was as far south as any road went. It was a long day up stream; we camped on an island and spent the next morning visiting several families. Ted Giles found that he had 14 school age children in just two families which were enough to start a public school. We came downriver in half a day and I remember it rained all the way home.

71

Travelling to the remote locations in winter was a real problem and it usually involved a joint expedition with the Indian Department bombardiers which were supposedly school buses but were used for everything but hauling kids to school. In the early winter of 1958, we made a trip to Fox Lake with the Indian Agent Ed Cousineau, the Roman Catholic Father Provincial and myself. I never got any

Fox Lake Hilton - 10 of us slept here one night

other name for him, but he was the overseer of all the Catholic churches in northern Alberta. I called him Father like everyone else and we got along fine. The two of us made many trips together, which gave us time to discuss the problems we both had in the area. He always had a bottle of Rye with him and I sometimes managed to save enough for a "Mickie" of rum, which came in handy when we had to shovel through a snowbank and found that his rye had frozen up in the back of the police truck. We had a good laugh over that, and I was quick to assure him that Anglicans drank rum because, like Hell, it never freezes.

Back to that first winter trip, we loaded up all the Indians' stuff and then stopped by the hospital to pick up "The Father" and all the church stuff. We had a pretty good load in the back with the extra gas, sleeping bags and the meager emergency supplies we carried. I never went on any long trips, winter or summer, without my trusty 303 rifle and a box of matches. On this occasion the only thing left behind was the packed lunch which the good Father forgot to pick up from the hospital. None of us had been down this winter road before, but we were assured that it was a wide enough road for the bombardier. I had looked at the width of the Indian freighter sleighs and was smart enough to borrow a chainsaw. It came in handy when we got stuck between two big spruce trees. We had to back up and cut one of them down. Backing up a bombardier with its long track and skis going backwards is not an easy task. The trip was otherwise uneventful, and I came back with another experience under my belt as I did all the driving.

A much more dangerous and stressful trip occurred later on when we had to do a forced TB evacuation from the Fox Lake area. This involved Jack Newman from the Indian Department and I was the enforcer. With no communications in the area it took a long time to get this all arranged and by the time we were ready to go the weather was colder than we had hoped. We got an early start and made the Fox Lake RC Mission around noon. We unloaded their supplies, including three fully charged 12-volt batteries. The patient was a young female but with the Father and a local interpreter we didn't think it was necessary to take along a matron. It was another 25 miles out to where the patient was located in a remote camp by a lake. We got stuck breaking road through the bushes onto the lake as nothing as big as a bombardier had ever been through that way before. When we did make it to the settlement there were only about three log cabins and the patient was in with a dozen persons of all ages – with most of them hacking and spitting. The negotiations then started which involved the Father and I explaining her disease and that everyone in the cabin would get sick and die if she didn't get treatment. I had a lot of empathy for her as many of the younger women that went out to the sanatorium in Edmonton did not come home. Some died and others ended up on the streets in the sex trade. She had refused to voluntarily go out for treatment, and I was not leaving without her so when she realized that "The Mountie" was going to take her if I had to throw her over my back and carry her out. She finally relented and with the clothes on her back and sobbing her heart out she climbed into the bombardier and we headed back to Fox Lake for the night. It was damn cold.

The bombardier was equipped with a propane heater to keep the engine warm. Jack and I lit it and waited for a few minutes to make sure it was working then crawled into our sleeping bags on the floor of the school room. We arose early next morning only to find that the propane line had frozen. We were stranded 80 miles from nowhere with an engine that would not start, as the starter would not even engage. Our answer was to build a fire under the bombardier - which we did. The engine was in the back and so was the gas tank. We started a small fire and as it melted into the snow, we just kept on adding more wood. We also covered the whole machine with tents, tarps and anything else we could find to keep the warmth in. By mid-afternoon and with the help of those 12-volt batteries and some ether from the nursing sister, we got the engine started only to find the tracks were frozen solid. We had to jack up one track to get the transmission turning. We then let the front end down and knocked the blocks out from under the back end with the one track turning – and voila we were on our way.

I took it for a little run and then came back to load up the TB patient and a nursing sister who was going "outside" and would act as matron. We opened out our sleeping bags and wrapped the two women up as best we could as it was still

Indian freight teams with wide sleighs

But not wide enough - we are STUCK

damn cold inside. We drove all the way home with one driving and one scraping the ice off the inside of the windshield. We made a quick stop at the Hudson's Bay Company and a Mennonite mission at Little Red River to see if anyone needed to go to the hospital or if there was anything else I had to attend to. Coming down we had wandered around on seismic lines but going home it was the shortest distance possible and that was up the river. As soon as we got above the rapids, we dropped down onto the river avoiding the winding road through the bush. We limped back onto land somewhere above the Wabasca River, picked up the sleigh road and from there it was only an hour or so to the edge of the farming district where we heaved a big sigh of relief. We stormed into the Fort about 3:00 in the morning, pried the nursing sister and our patient out of the bombardier and into the hospital. Jack dropped me off and took the machine home to his farm. I had to wake Helen up to let me in, checked the three oil stoves to see they had oil and were running on high and crawled into bed. Another routine patrol.

We knew it was cold as the mercury in the thermometer at Fox Lake was all in the bulb and none was showing in the stem, which meant it was around 60 degrees celsius below. It was not until long after I retired and was playing around with my computer that I learned that it was some of the coldest weather ever recorded in North America – the third week in March 1959. Looking back on it now I consider leaving the safety of the Mission at Fox Lake was the DUMBEST THING I did in my whole RCMP career. We should have stayed at Fox Lake with the motor running all night and left at daylight the next day. I guess common sense went out the window and I was thinking only of a pregnant wife and two small boys alone in a cold ten room house with five stoves to keep running. If that bombardier had stopped or if we had broken down no one would know where we were at or that we were in serious trouble. As the youngest and fittest one I would have had to strap on my snowshoes and go for help. At that temperature I would not likely have made more than about five miles, the outcome would have been disastrous, and this story would not have had a good ending. Not a pleasant thought.

Fort Vermilion is the only place I was stationed that I did not have a Boy Scout troop or some connection with the Boy Scout movement. There were no scouts in Fort Vermilion – in fact there were no sports of any kind for the younger generation. We built a one sheet curling rink, but it was on a swampy piece of land and only lasted for a year or two. There was a weekly 16mm movie shown in the village hall and that was about the only entertainment. There was the odd dance in the hall but not on a regular basis. The lack of any operating and effective civic authority was definitely a drawback to the vibrancy of the community.

There was one other trip that could be somewhat of an adventure and that was into Habay or Hay Lakes. The trail ran west for about 60 miles from Meander River on the Mackenzie Highway. The first 20 miles were on a graded dirt road, the middle 20 through a heavy forest of spruce and poplar and the last 20 across a grassy swamp. I made my first trip with Sgt. Chris Christianson who had been stationed in the Fort in the early 1950's. He was then stationed in Red Deer and brought with him a couple of Chinese restaurant owners going on a goose hunt. I would not have made it without his insistence that the road was actually used in the summer. The bush section was merely a series of mud holes and required a great deal of winching. On a later trip it took me 27 hours to go the 60 miles. On that first trip we came upon a BIG beaver dam and the only way across was to line up one wheel on each side of the dam, put the vehicle in neutral and winch it across. With water on one side and a 12-foot drop on the other I was more than a little puckered up on that first crossing. Habay was no more than a HBC post, an Indian Agent and a few native houses. About ten miles west of there, in the Zama Lake area, was a three story Roman Catholic Indian School. Most of the students were local but a few were boarded at the school. This was a relatively new building with its own light, water and sewer. There was a red headed Irish Priest in charge, and I stayed with him on some of my winter trips. Not only did he have all the comforts of civilization, but he had the best stocked liquor cabinet north of Edmonton. Helen was not at all impressed when I came home and told her "I had had a bath." We were still living in a house not fit for the Indians.

When we got to Hay Lakes there were 14 private aircraft sitting on the dirt runway. All but two were Americans. I checked a few hunters just to let them know that they were in Canada and that they played by our rules. There were geese by the millions but without dogs to retrieve them from the water they were not that easy to shoot. It was there that I first saw an old Native hunting with an HBC double barrel percussion cap 26 gauge shotgun. Four geese came over and he shot two, then he kept cackling with only his mouth, called back the same geese as he stoked up the muzzle loader. The other two geese came back over him and he shot them both. I was wailing away with a 12-gauge shotgun and couldn't hit anything. It took me two and half years to talk him into selling me that gun, but I did get it in the end. It is now hanging in my den with David's name on it.[7] It was at Habay (Hay Lakes) where a native lady, Elizabeth Chocklay, made me a pair of mukluks with moose hide bottoms and caribou leg tops. She also made two wonderful pairs of unsmoked deer hide gauntlets for myself and Helen. Mine got a little wet and hardened up but Helen's are in perfect condition and up for grabs.

There was a very severe rabies epidemic in northern Alberta in the mid-1950 and there were still remnants of it around when I arrived in Fort Vermilion. At first, I did not believe the horror stories of Timberwolves biting onto rubber tractor tires and the farmer killing them with an iron bar when they came up to the top of the wheel. Apparently, they would not or could not let go of the rubber. I found this was true and at other times when wolves tried to break into a house or barn. The Mennonites had no guns; the women held the door shut on the inside with rabid wolves snarling on the outside. I soon got the message that if any animal, tame or wild was acting strange - shoot it. I started carrying my shotgun around the settlement areas and did shoot dogs, coyotes, foxes and even rabbits. The forestry service was still doing aircraft drops of horse meat laced with cyanide in remote areas. The epidemic was pretty much over it by the time I left.

Sometime in late 1958 a buzz went through the Force that Prime Minister John Diefenbaker was building new RCMP Offices all over Canada. It was a day of celebration when it was confirmed that Fort Vermilion was on the list for a new building. The building was completed in late 1959 and with it came a new power plant and a proper electrical grid. Of course they located the new diesel plant a block away from our backyard. We had electricity but we also had the noise. I also got a second man which meant I was due for promotion. It was a happy day when I could move my wife and family back into civilized accommodation with central heat, flush toilets and water that came out of taps.

7. Upon publishing of this book, the gun has now been passed down to my granddaughter, David's youngest, Kimberly Louise.

Fort Vermilion

The nearest plumber was 250 miles away so on my next trip out to Peace River the first thing I did was pick up a couple of pipe wrenches. The water was from a well and when tested it was supposedly the hardest water in Canada. A stupid soft water system was installed for the house and singles men's residence, but not for the prisoner's sink. The water softener had a 300-gallon tank and took 100 lbs. of salt every time it had to recycle. They had to tear out part of the walls to re-plumb a lot of the house and I had a salt mine in the basement.

Of course, the O.C. in Peace River could not see me too happy so on January 1st, 1960 I was off to Regina for a six-week Junior NCO's Training course. Taking the course was okay but it meant I was again leaving Helen and now three little boys alone in the middle of winter. My first Cst. was Bernie Lowe and he was just out of training so before Christmas they moved him and brought in Cst. Dal Langenberger. He had about five years of service and was to keep things running while I was away. The new building had steam heat with an oil-fired burner, but you had to have water, electricity and oil or there was no heat.

Fort Vermilion may have been my most interesting posting, but it was certainly not the most rewarding. To start with we were living in a dilapidated, run down mansion of a house that was unfit for human occupation and had none of the comforts of a civilized dwelling. I was alone, had no communication what-so-ever with the outside world and for the first eight months was without even a Police vehicle and I was the lucky one. A billion words and 100 books could not cover all that Helen contributed to our three year stay in isolation – and she never once complained. Whenever I had a prisoner, which was not too often, Helen was expected to provide the meals at a princely sum of $.25 per meal. They got the same food as we did and on occasion joined us at the table. Most of my prisoners were trustees and were only locked in at night. They often split wood and did chores around the place rather than sit in the cell. Sometimes I even took them with me in the truck when I was driving around, and I never worried about them escaping. There was no place to go. I don't think I ever had one native in the cell who did not want to thank Helen for her care and meals when they left, whether going home or going to jail. They would ask me if they could thank Mrs. Elliott and would come into the kitchen and do so in a very polite and sincere manner.

The second winter we were at the Fort Helen began substitute teaching at the Indian residential school. She soon developed a good rapport with a couple of the teaching sisters. She invited them down for tea and on the first couple of occasions Father Tessier felt he had to accompany them. However, it was not long before the sisters were visiting on their own. Our one and only Doctor, Doug Cassidy, was an Irish Roman Catholic and the sisters could not or would not visit his wife which caused a bit of jealousy over Helen's visits. Father Tessier taught the daily catechism but after a month or so he said to Helen "You're Anglican and know the catechism as well as I do, so from now on you teach it." Helen quite enjoyed singing in English while the sisters sang in Latin. Needless to say, with Helen's charm and personality there were a whole lot of little Indian kids in love with Mrs. Elliott. When the new building was completed, we had the Indian school kids down for a visit. All the girls wanted to do was to see the house where Mrs. Elliott lived, and the boys wanted to see the jail.

When Helen was substituting, we had a Metis neighbour lady by the name of Mrs. Sanderson over to babysit. I never did know her given name. She was raised in a Catholic convent and certainly knew how to cook and keep house. The kids loved her and so did I as every time she babysat, she made fresh buns. She would never use the propane stove oven but preferred the big old six-hole wood stove. She would test the oven temperature with her elbow and if too hot she would prop the oven door open with a piece of wood and the whole house, including my office, smelled like a bakery. When we moved to Uxbridge Drive in Calgary, she had a daughter living a few blocks down the street. She spent more time with Helen than with her daughter, claiming she felt more at home with us.

Like any family with kids there are always a few traumatic moments that give us grey hairs far too soon. Unfortunately, Helen was frequently alone when our scary adventures happened. One of Danny, my oldest son's adventures may not have been the first one, but it certainly proves that he started his fishing at an early date. I was away and he was supposedly outside playing in the yard with an Indian boy about the same age when he came home all excited to tell his mother about the BIG fish they caught. I don't know where the string and fishhook came from but the two of them had gone across the road, down to the river, and indeed did catch a fish. Getting it out of the water was apparently the adventurous part. About the time Helen was ready to start warming up Danny's bottom as he was relaying the grey-hairing adventurous story he said, "Mummy I gave him the fish because that's all they have to eat you know." Danny, you have always been a kind and thoughtful person.

David, my middle son's adventures started when he was about two. We were visiting an assistant Indian Agent on the Boyer Indian Reserve which was on the north side of the river. About the time our host called us to dinner there was an emergent banging on the door as some kid had cut his foot with an axe. The agent and I went to check him out and sure enough he had cut his foot really bad and needed surgery immediately. We had to bandage him up and take him over to the hospital, which meant a ferry ride each way. During all the confusion and excitement David, who was lying on a bed in the bedroom somehow got into a purse, found a bottle of aspirin, and proceeded to eat a bunch. We don't know how many he got before his big brother told Helen what was going on. We had the only car and there was nothing the girls could do but get Dave to throw up and fill him full of milk. The pills didn't seem to bother Dave too much, he just had a good sleep. It sure put stress on Helen to be on the wrong side of the river, away from the hospital and with no car. As soon as I got back with the car, we headed back across the river, so we'd be near the hospital. The dinner party was delayed for another time.

David's next adventure was when I was down river paying treaty. Helen was visiting the Cassidy's who had two girls about the same age as our boys. Once again Danny came and alerted Mummy that David had swallowed a penny. Helen said that couldn't be because he didn't have any, but oh yes, he'd found one on the floor. Of course, the only place a kid can put anything is in their mouth and he had indeed swallowed the penny. Off to the hospital, where x-rays revealed it was going to his lungs and not into his stomach. This was serious and if it went into his lungs, we would have to get him flown out to Edmonton on a Police plane as soon as possible. All night long Helen kept his feet elevated and watched his breathing. In the morning a second x-ray revealed the penny was now in his stomach and it was little blue potty for a couple of days until the penny showed up.

With no fire departments most two-story buildings in the olden days had an escape ladder from the second floor. Ours in the police building was out the bedroom window, onto the kitchen and down a ladder. Our neighbour had a two-story building with the ladder going up onto the roof by a dormer window. This was too much for an adventurous spirit like David's and he crawled all the way up to the top of the ladder then like a cat, couldn't come down. I don't know whether Danny talked him into going up or not, but it was once again Danny who had to go to Mummy for help. Helen came out and all she could do was plead with David to hang on while she sent Danny to find somebody, anybody. Danny ran over to Mrs. Anderson's house (the babysitter) and got her son to come and rescue Dave. The said son was the town drunk and Helen made it quite clear that under no circumstances was he ever to be arrested or put in the cell again or she would let him go and lock me up. I took her at her word.

Lee, my youngest son's first adventure was not of his own making. He was born with a groin hernia and his intestine would pop out all on its own. Dr. Cassidy had been too long in Africa and said something to the effect "Oh that's nothing, you just take your finger like this and squish it back in." That was not to our liking and as soon as I could get holidays we headed for Grand Prairie and the Doctor who delivered Danny and David. He took one look at Lee and said, "This child should never have left the hospital, I'll operate this afternoon." Unfortunately, that would not work as we were meeting Helen's Mum and Dad at the train station in Edmonton the next morning. They were returning from a trip to Nova Scotia and there was no way of contacting them. No problem, Dr. Tredegar arranged for surgery at the Misericordia hospital in Edmonton at 8:00 a.m. the next morning. We were all at the hospital at 7:30, Helen stayed with her baby and the boys and I picked up Frank and Sarah. The real stress came when we learned that the hernia could have strangulated at any time and death would've followed within hours. Living in an isolated community with no communications with the outside world was not for the faint of heart.

Lee had one more little adventure while I was at my training course in Regina. He managed somehow to get his head stuck between the first railing and the headboard of his crib. When Helen found him, he was stuck, and she could not get his head back inside. Once again it was Danny to the rescue. She sent him down to wake up Cst. Langenberger in the single man's quarters to get upstairs with a screwdriver - right now. Dal loosened off the headboard and Lee was extracted with no problem. I don't know what would've happened if Dal had been away, but I am sure Helen would've figured something out. It was another stressful moment she didn't need. Dal was not my favourite Cst., but once again Helen had another "Hero" whom I had to treat with unearned respect.

The boys were not the only ones to add to Helen's grey hair. I added a few with my night's away, not getting back as planned and with no communication to let her know I was alright. The more serious mishaps happened as a result of a Government decision that I still cannot comprehend. I was in the office of our new building in the late fall of 1959 when the delivery truck started backing up the driveway. I went out to see what was going on and was mystified to find he was dropping off about 1500 to 2000 pounds of canned spam - cases upon cases of the bloody stuff. It wasn't until several days later that I got a memo from Sub/Division advising that the ham was provided by the provincial government and I was to deliver it to anyone in need. Real police work? After a couple of months, we were tired of all those boxes in the office so we would load up the truck drive, around the communities and drop off a box to anyone in need. Once we were on a trip out towards High Level when we were told that a bachelor may need some assistance. We tried to drive to his house and got ourselves stuck in the snow about 50 yards off the highway. I had the truck jacked up and was underneath putting on chains while my Cst. shovelled us out. He had never shovelled snow in his life, however, he was enthusiastic, so much so that he knocked the jack over, and I was pinned under the truck. Fortunately, the snow was fairly soft, and nothing was broken but I was bruised all over. It just so happened that Helen was giving a talk to the sisters and staff at the residential school that night and I had to get home. We left the truck stuck and caught a ride back to town. I don't know if the frozen ham was any good, but I was happy to see the last box go out the door. I was rather black and blue and bruised all over for a while, but nothing was broken and after a little TLC I was back to normal. Another bad decision escaped!!

Wayne Wright, the seed farmer, thought that the soil and climate in the area was perfect for growing potatoes. In the spring of 1959, he planted a few acres and ended up with a bumper crop. He stored them over winter in a root cellar dug into the riverbank. In the spring of 1960 potatoes were selling at $.14 a pound in the isolated communities of the north. Wayne, Hank Anderson from the experimental farm, his hired man, and myself set off on a "spud flight." We flew to Fort Smith, Fort Resolution, Yellowknife, Fort Providence, Hay River and back to Fort Vermilion in two days. He had enough orders for potatoes to hire a DC3 and fly them into all the above areas before spring break up. I got in a few hours of flying lessons and had a very welcome home. Helen opened the door, held out her arms and with a big smile on her face said,"Welcome home Cpl. Elliott." I had been promoted.

Cochrane

On May 9, 1960 I got more good news, in the mail, that I was being transferred to Cochrane, Alberta. The only thing I knew about Cochrane Detachment was that it was at the bottom of a big hill west of Calgary and the trucks had a habit of running into the barracks. It made no difference where we were moving; we were going back to civilization. I had holidays coming so took them first and did not take over Cochrane detachment until August 30, 1960.

The Mounted Police were known for having crappy accommodation for both members and family. It was no surprise then when I got to Cochrane and found that the barracks were an old Alberta Provincial Police (APP) building. The APP was formed in 1918 as there were insufficient RNWMP (Royal North West Mounted Police) available as most were overseas in WWI. They were disbanded in 1932 at the beginning of the Great Depression and their members were absorbed into the RCMP. The building was just a little bungalow with two bedrooms, kitchen, bath and living room. The office was located in one front corner of the building. It was small with a steel cell, one four drawer file cabinet, a desk and a couple of chairs. The cell was on the other side of the living room wall, which was the only place we could put our chesterfield. The phone system was centrally operated through an operator and the only phone was in the office with an extension to the kitchen. Communications had a way to go, but it was a huge improvement over being stuck up in the bush.

My predecessor had moved a week before I got to Cochrane and things were being held together by a young Cst. by the name of Bob Charlesworth.

Consequently, I was unable to get any first-hand information as to the policing of Cochrane or what major files were still open. It didn't take me too long to learn that Charlesworth was afraid to leave the office and every file he had investigated was merely a "typewriter patrol." I soon had him shipped back to Calgary and he was replaced by a couple of farm boys from, British Columbia, Al Loshny and John Moller. They turned out to be two of the best members I had during my entire service. They both came off farms near Salmon Arm, BC, and were inquisitive, intuitive and determined investigators. Al didn't stay with me too long as John was one of the first members to get married under the three years of service requirement and Cochrane was considered a suitable posting for a married man. His wife Mabel and Helen became good friends, with Helen being her mentor during their five year stay in Cochrane. Unfortunately, John died early of ALS and I was honoured to do his eulogy at a huge memorial in Red Deer. Mabel lives in BC and we still keep in contact after more than fifty years.

I had a third man on the Cochrane Detachment - an Indian by the name of Moses Ear. He lived on the Morley Reserve and was on the RCMP books as an Indian Scout. He was the last Indian Scout in the Mounted Police and served for a full 20 years, receiving an RCMP pension. Other native employees were called Special Cst.'s and had some form of police uniform. Moses was a big help to me as he knew everyone on the Reserve, where to find them and what they were up to. He could also be a nuisance and frequently if we were having a party he would show up with a drunk, once his own son, and we would have to run the prisoner into the guard room in Calgary. He was also a great tracker as was demonstrated when someone broke into a bachelor's ranch house and stole a tobacco can full of money. Moses wandered off into the bush and didn't come back for an hour but when he showed up, he had a smile on his face and was unfortunately using the tobacco can like a basketball - so much for fingerprints. He tracked the culprit, obviously another Indian, for over a mile through the bush and dry grass. It was a feat to be admired but added little to the investigation. I was the first one to let him drive the marked police car around the Reserve and that elevated his status considerably. We had a Caragana hedge around the detachment and I had him tidy it up each spring. We would have him for dinner and he enjoyed it so much that he started bringing his wife Virginia in to help. I didn't mind that except I was a little miffed when they got their morning coffee served in china cups and saucers while I got a mug. Helen knew "my place" and we carried this tradition on until our office was moved to new quarters.

In 1960 Cochrane was still a farm and ranching community so I felt right at home. I joined the Masonic Lodge, got active in scouts and we attended the Anglican Church, which was right across the street from the office. Danny started school, Helen got to meet the teachers and within a month we were part of the community. When moving into a new community you had to be careful about accepting invitations, as you may find yourself with the wrong crowd. This also held true for the wives, so it was several weeks before Helen got to go solo on her first visit, which was to Annie Raby's. Annie and Ed ran the Esso bulk fuel plant and Annie was a bit of a character – sometimes referred to as "Tugboat Annie", but not to her face. Helen was only gone long enough for me to get the kids to bed when the fire siren went off. Within seconds the phone rang, and the operator informed me the fire was at Newt Gilbert's ranch. Without thinking I said, "I have no babysitter" and just as fast the operator said, "I'll be right over." I threw on a pair of pants, my leather jacket, and forage hat. A sixteen-year-old girl ran in the front door and all I told her was "There're three boys in there" pointing to the bedroom. I didn't even know her name. When Helen came home, she was told that I had gone to a fire. The young lady would not consider taking any pay, insisting that your husband had to go to work. It was a warm welcome into the social, caring, community of Cochrane. An opinion we held throughout our seven-year stay.

Helen worked as a telephone operator in Peace River before our marriage and I knew that they often listened in on conversations. I realized in Cochrane what a great asset those operators were for a local Policeman. Often when I would make a call to somebody or a household they would say, they are not home they are at so and so's place, I'll put you through. They were also part of the police service as every prairie town that had both a water tower and a police detachment had a red light on top of the tower. Whenever I was out of the office and needed, the operators would turn on the red light and I would call in to pick up the message. A telephone operator had to do something really awful before they got in my bad books. It was more likely that a replaced headlight or a flat tire repair on my expense account would end up as a box of chocolates in the telephone office.

We got a babysitter and spent our first New Year's Eve party at Newt and Betty Gilbert's place where we met more local ranchers. Helen duly noted that I was the only one present without cowboy boots. At her insistence that was rectified on Boxing Day when I bought my first pair of snakeskin cowboy boots from the British Boot store. I wore those boots to both Europe and Australia; plus, our square dancing five nights a week and they were still in great shape until my feet would longer fit in them. With them I fit right in with the Cochrane cowboy culture.

In the spring of 1961, I accepted invitations to a couple of branding bees, one at Richard Butters and another on the south side of the river at Percy Copithorne's. Thank God I did the one at Richard Butters place first as I had a lot to learn. They had a smaller herd and it was much more relaxed. Two of the older Cowboys would ride slowly into the herd, flick their lariat once, have a calf by a hind leg and drag it into the branding pen. Then all we had to do was hold it down, doctor up the males, give them an injection, notch one ear and burn on the brand. We branded all morning and then it was beer, dinner and story time.

Within a week I was invited over to a branding at the Copithorne's and that was something else. They had all their calves corralled, YOU grabbed one by the hind leg and YOU dragged it into the branding pen. They had four fire pits, many irons and the place was a chaotic zoo. They put through hundreds of calves and by noon my butt was dragging. But here again it was beer, dinner and more stories. The end result of these two brandings was that I was known to most of the ranchers in the area. I had held my own when it came to getting down and dirty and was somebody they could trust. Those two brandings paid off in spades during my following years of policing that area as no policeman had done that in the last thirty years.

Branding at Copithorne's

By the summer of 1961 with my lodge, church, Scouts, school patrol and merchants in Bragg Creek, Morley and Bottrel, I had friends or contacts in every quadrant of my area. There were a few bad dudes around that I had to keep an eye on but I was policing my way - "Everyone was a good, law abiding citizen and my job was not to harass them, but keep them safe." My biggest problem was the proximity to the city of Calgary and the fact that the Cochrane bar had mixed drinking. Beer parlors in Calgary were segregated with men and women having their own rooms. The foothills and mountains were also a big draw to young romantics who wanted to find a secluded place to drink beer and do whatever else young people did. This resulted in a lot of liquor seizures as the ranchers did not like glass bottles left on their land. In my seven years at Cochrane there were a few backseat date rapes reported but I don't think any of these ever made it to trial.

I soon learned that ranchers only get mad if their machinery or anything else was stolen but if a critter disappeared – that was a hanging offence. So, when cattle started being shot with a bow and arrow, then only one hind quarter removed, the whole district was up in arms. John Moller and I could only do so many night patrols but thanks to Clarence Copithorne, the local MLA, a second Cst. was added to the detachment. When a calf was found with an arrow through its neck it gave me our first clue. Arrows are marked and sold by the dozen and there was only one archery store in Calgary at that time. When I showed up with the broken arrow the reaction in the store told me that they damn well knew who had purchased those arrows. It might even have been one of their own employees. I didn't solve the case, but the archery hunting stopped.

I found that policing next to a major city was far different than what I was used to in northern Alberta. Aside from the usual problems with Indian Reserves, 80% of the crime committed in my area was by outsiders. My problems were also compounded by having the Spy Hill jail in my area as at that time it was outside the city limits. There was always a prisoner or two making a run for the city. The city police usually picked them up on Spy Hill or in the Brentwood area. At that time the jail had a farm attached with a good-sized dairy herd and a large garden. The labor for these was provided by trustees and it was a good program as most prisoners preferred to be working rather than locked in their cell. The milk, cream and garden products were used in the jail kitchen, providing healthy fresh food.

With freedom comes opportunities and one of the problems with the farm was that the prisoners were always working on some scheme to make home brew. The warden was after me to help him solve this problem and my opinion was that, "I put them in jail. You can look after them." I did suggest that they put something in the brew that would make them so sick they would never try it again. This led to the Assistant Warden Slim Adair coming up with a brilliant idea. Slim lived in Cochrane, was in Lodge and a good friend of mine. When it became obvious that two of the ringleaders were sampling their product, Slim and the Warden stopped them, and the conversation went something like this. "How's that homebrew coming along that you have in the barn loft behind the hay bales?" This let them know that the brew had been found and they said something to the effect – "How did you know that." Slim replied "Hell we've been pissing in your brew for the last two days." Problem solved. The farm project was eventually closed because there were too many do-gooders complaining about the poor prisoners having to do all that hard work. Plus, the city wanted the land.

As a way to rehabilitate trustworthy prisoners and keep the program going the province set up a bush camp on the Forestry Road near Wapiti Creek. This was no more than a few trailers and they were far too close to the main road. The prisoners could roam free for a mile in any direction and could be away for up to two hours at any one time. It soon became known as "The jail and tail camp." The prisoner's girlfriends would have somebody drop them off with a blanket and a case of beer and pick them up an hour or so later. The prisoner would return to camp happy, smiling and sometimes drunk. Of course, the odd prisoner thought why just an hour, I can be back in Calgary before I'm missed. Another escaped prisoner for me to deal with! Fortunately, this camp did not last long and was disbanded after the second summer.

The Cochrane detachment boundaries were somewhat fluid. They went from the city limits to the Kananaskis River bridge on the TransCanada Highway, south past Bragg Creek (or the Highwood Pass) and north to Cremona. But when it came to going north on the Forestry Trunk road there was no boundary. When I was in the north and a hunter did not return it was a serious matter and a concern for everyone. I was not prepared for the idiotic, stupid and just plain dumb hunters that got lost in the area northwest of Cochrane. My first year in Cochrane I experienced several "lost Hunter" cases only to find out the wife did not know where her husband might be hunting, what he was hunting, who with or what vehicle he was driving. The next year I developed a new policy; day one do-nothing, day two, take down details and day three start searching. It saved a whole lot of work and frustration.

After a night lost in the bush, they usually found a way out on their own. They would also be a whole lot smarter and better prepared next time.

I had one memorable search not for a hunter, but for a lost cowhand. Two twenty-year olds, Sylvio Levelle (Cowboy Joe) and Norman St. Jacques came west from Ontario with one purpose in mind to become Cowboys and have some excitement. It ended up that they made history, but it was not too exciting for them. They got work with the D.V. Chapman Ranch and were sent into the Fallen Timber to round up cattle in the summer grazing area. They spent four weeks in a tent and were about ready to call it quits when Cowboy Joe spotted some cattle in a coulee. He left on his own to round them up and it would be four days before Norman saw his friend again. It snowed that night and Norman searched all the next day before riding out to phone his boss - and that's where I came in.

John Moller and I, with Ray Hill and Ernie Pisikla of the Alberta Forestry Service, led the search in two Jeeps. We had sixteen cowboys, plus construction and oil field workers join us with vehicles of all sorts. By dark we had not found so much as a track and with new fallen snow it looked pretty bleak. The search resumed next morning, and I chartered a plane to assist from the air. Ray Hill and I hunted in that area and I was familiar with most of it and able to direct them to the best ground routes. I kept expanding my search area and eventually spotted a single horse track on a cutline about 15 miles from their line camp. I relayed this information to Cst. John Moller who then directed Ray and Ernie to the site. They found Cowboy Joe lying under a large tree still holding onto the reins of his horse. He was curled up in a ball trying to keep warm. All he had on was a pair of jeans and a tattered T-shirt. He had gotten lost in the snowstorm on the first night and was hoping to get enough energy back to get on his horse and ride out. It is doubtful if he would have survived another night without shelter. He spent a few days in hospital but suffered no lasting ill effects. As I told the press Cowboy Joe was one tough man." His story made the national press and so did Cpl. Elliott.

With thousands of head of cattle running at large, thefts were a major problem in the Cochrane area. There were large grazing leases all along the foothills where cattle were left on their own during the summer months. With 39,000 registered cattle brands in Alberta we relied heavily on the Provincial Brand Inspectors working at both rural auctions and slaughterhouses. The greatest number of cattle went through the Burns slaughterhouse and stock yards in south east Calgary. There were always several Brand Inspectors on duty and that's where we got a lot of our rustling tips. Ranchers with between 500 and a thousand heads don't miss one or two and the thefts usually come to light when somebody tries to convert the cattle into cash. I had a couple of cases that started when a dumb crook stole two unbranded calves from a farmyard. The Brand Inspectors caught them as he sold them in his own name. When I arrested and questioned him extensively, he was looking for some leniency and dropped a hint about someone else who had stolen five heads of cattle off a ranch. These were sold at auction in Olds, Alberta. We had a Sub/Division stock man, Cpl. George Offley and between us we were able to track down and identify the person who made the sale. The courtroom in Cochrane was packed full when the two suspects appeared before our lay Magistrate, Arthur Court. I was prosecuting and guilty pleas were entered. I not only presented the facts but went on to explain how difficult it was for ranchers to protect their free ranging cattle. Cattle thefts were on the increase and they had to be stopped. I deliberately set the two cases on the same day to emphasize the rash of thefts occurring in my area. Magistrate Court picked up on this and after some stern lectures he sentenced the one who stole the five heads to two years less a day in jail. The one who stole the two calves got 18 months. Everyone but the two crooks were happy, and I was a hero for the day.

I have one more cattle rustling story to tell and it's the one that is most unique. It also gave me the most satisfaction. Shortly after my first branding sessions, a couple of ranchers informed me about a local by the name of Jack L------ (he still has family living in Cochrane and I don't want to taint the kid's with their father's crimes) was stealing horses and cattle off the Morley Indian Reserve. Livestock on a Reserve do not belong to the Indians, but to the Federal Government, and laying a charge under those circumstances was futile. I checked Jack a number of times, but he never sold anything with a brand on it. Then one morning I got a call from the Brand Inspectors in Calgary that someone had brought in a Holstein male calf and they were suspicious of the circumstances. When told that it was Jack L------ I said, "It's stolen." I phoned my dairy farmers contact, Gordon Bowhay, and told him if it was not his, to start calling his neighbours. Time was of the essence, so I called a few myself, then sat back to wait for the phone to ring. Within an hour I got a call from a farmer north east of Cochrane. He was uncertain whether he'd lost a calf or not but had an old cow who was bawling her head off and was upset about something. Taking a chance, I told him to gather all his cattle, including the calves into his corral, then put the bawling cow as far from the gate as possible. I then called the Brand Inspectors and had them bring the calf out to the farmer's place, where I would meet them. They let the calf out at the gate and when it started bawling, the cow started heading through the herd like a dose of salts. You could almost hear her saying, "Get out of my way, I want my baby." She gave the calf one lick, it immediately started suckling and the old cow stopped bawling. The two Brand Inspectors, and everyone else there said, "That calf belongs to that cow." A cow will only allow her own offspring to suckle. I had my owner for a stolen calf. I laid a charge of theft of cattle, got a warrant and arrested Jack before the day was out. He opted for a jury trial, was convicted and sentenced to jail. I forget how much time he got, but it made no difference. After a lot of false starts, I had put another cattle thief behind bars. The case was well reported in the local press and my community support went up a notch.

I investigated and prosecuted a lot of fairly serious criminal cases during my time in Cochrane. I succeeded, not necessarily because I was so smart, but because frequently, crooks are dumb. The first case happened shortly after I got to Cochrane. It involved a man travelling alone across Canada. He stopped for supper at the Calgary bus depot and picked up four young hitchhikers heading west. Just before Scott Lake hill, they decided to rob him. They beat him up, took his clothes, tied his feed together with his own belt and dumped him in the ditch. It didn't take him long to get loose and the only light he could see was the flare from the Shell oil gas plant. Instead of waiting for someone to come by he struck off, across the country to the gas plant. I got a call from there about 1:00 in the morning. Since the thieves were heading west, I called Banff Detachment to set up a checkpoint at the Park gate. To my delight, a rookie Cst., on his very first night of working alone said, "I think I got them. I didn't like their story, so told them to follow me into the office." I told you they were dumb!

I took the victim with me and by the time we got to Banff, the Sgt. was on the scene and had the four suspects in separate cells, mixed with other prisoners. The victim walked by the cells and identified all four suspects. Charges of robbery with violence were laid. Magistrate A.G. Court was called, trials were held and each elected trial by Magistrate alone. Guilty pleas were entered and after informing them that their crimes were heinous acts in the sight of God and man, he sentenced each to five years in the Prince Albert Penitentiary. The Detachment secretary typed out the necessary exhibit reports for me to return all his possessions back to the victim. I had breakfast with the Sgt. and by then, the necessary imprisonment documents had been prepared and signed. I borrowed a couple of pairs of handcuffs, put one cuffed prisoner in the front and the other three, double cuffed, in the back seat, and headed for Calgary. I dropped the prisoners off at the Sub/Division Guardroom and was home in time for lunch.

After about five years through my stay in Cochrane, the province eliminated Lay Magistrates like Arthur Court. They then appointed lawyers throughout the province as Judicial Magistrates. At the same time, they decided that policemen should not be prosecuting their own cases and appointed a batch of lawyers as provincial prosecutors. Some of these appointees had no court experience whatsoever. I remember sitting with one such prosecutor at a jury trial and I had to help him pick the jurors. The trial was over some rural theft, so if the prospective juror did not have callused hands and an outdoor complexion, we stood him aside. The defence lawyer was just as new, didn't realize what I was doing, and the poor accused was guilty before the trial started. A few months after this transition to all Lawyer Magistrates, I was talking to an Elder from the Morley Reserve. After much thought, he summed up the new court system with this wise observation, "Lots more law, but not as much justice." I fully agreed with him, and it was one of the most profound comments I've ever heard.

There was a Kerrfoot & Downs hardware store on the Main Street of Cochrane and Roy Downs lived above the store with his family. I got a call from Roy in the middle of the night advising that the store was broken into and the culprits were still inside. I gave John (Cst. Moller) a quick call and told him to take the front street and I'd take the alley where the entry point would likely be located. I leaped through the broken window, pistol in hand, and crashed onto the floor with a thud that shook the whole building. Roy came down, turned on the lights and a quick check revealed that the crooks had fled the premises. We had recently received portable radios and when I called John and his reply was "I got them." How many? "All of them." How many is ALL? "Four." Roy let me out of the store and there came John down the street with four prisoners marching in front of him, still carrying their loot. We secured the stolen property in the store for later indexing and walked the prisoners back to the office. I don't remember the names of the two 20-year olds, but I certainly remember the 16-year-old Smith twins.

The next day, a very timid and distressed young lady came into the office and asked if I remembered her, to which I had to reply "no." In a very trembling voice, she whispered. I'm Jimmie Smith's daughter from White Fish Lake. My heart stopped. James Smith was the Hudson's Bay factor at Atikameg (known locally as White Fish Lake) and I had stayed with them on many occasions when on patrol from High Prairie. The daughter would have been about ten and the twins about 3 or 4 at the time. I remember how excited they were when I showed up in uniform, them jumping all over me and I telling them bedtime stories. I don't remember what I said but I immediately found myself with a shaking, sobbing young lady in my arms, who could not get herself under control. I finally took her into the house where Helen sat with her until she gained her composure. The story came out that Jim had died, and the mother brought the family to Calgary where she found employment in the HBC drapery department. The twins had seldom been to a town let alone to a large city and soon fell in with the wrong crowd - although this was their first run in with the law.

I had to inform Miss Smith that it was impossible to withdraw the charges and that her brothers would have to go to court. They of course could not afford a lawyer, but I assured her that I would do absolutely everything in my power to see that they got the most lenient sentence possible. The sentencing options of the present time were not available in the 1960's. A break and entry conviction meant you were heading to jail. Magistrate Arthur Court heard the case and I was the prosecutor, presenting the evidence much as I have related above. I don't remember any of the sentences, but I expect the twins would get a month or less and the ringleaders at least six months. This seemingly routine investigation and subsequent court case reveals that sometimes a successful conviction can be just as stressful as rewarding. I can still hear that big sister crying over the fate of her younger brothers and I wish I could've done things differently. With today's court options I'm sure those two misguided young boys would not have gone to jail, which is just a training centre for other illegal activities. I was too busy with work and family to keep track of the Smiths' and I never heard from them again.

Cochrane was not all doom and gloom Police work and it was a great place to raise a family. Danny started school in the fall of 1960 and his teacher was a kind loving grandma by the name of Voila McPherson. She taught all three boys Grade 1 and although she was strict and not above turning a misbehaving child over her knee for a few pats on the bum, she got every student in Cochrane off to a good start. Lee started Grade 1 with her grandson and even he got into trouble if he called her "Grandma" in class. She was either "Teacher or Mrs. McPherson." They were an old Cochrane family with grown children and a big part of the town's history. The "Cop's and Ministers kids" usually got picked on at school but with my involvement in Scouts and School Patrol this did not happen in Cochrane. Within a few months I knew every kid in town and they all knew me.

With my love of boating and fishing I decided that with a family of boys we needed a boat The only problem was boats

Launching our boat at Ghost Lake for a Sunday outing

were beyond our disposable income and so I   Launching our boat at Ghost Lake for a Sunday outing decided to build one myself. I bought a 16-foot molded plywood hull with the transom installed and finished the rest myself. By the second summer we had a nice safe boat, with a 40 HP motor and a custom-made trailer built by a shop in Calgary. With a small tent and a few sleeping bags we were ready to set off on some great adventures. Our first big trip was to Salmon Arm and free parking with John Moller's parents. The highway through Roger Pass was not yet open so we had to go by the Big Ben highway between Golden and Revelstoke. This was a 150-mile loop along the Columbia River on a gravel road through a forest of trees. With the trees there was no wind and it was dust, dust and more dust all the way at a very limited speed. We didn't make it all the way the first day and had to stop at dusk and set up our tent. We stayed at the Moller's for a few days where the kids could play in the barn loft and pick cattails in the ditches. We then moved to a campground along a canal at the bottom end of Kalamalka Lake. This was a perfect place for the boys. I water skied and we all ate cherries and peaches right off the trees. Coming back John's Dad had "a few things" to send home with me. Those few things turned out to be gunny sacks of corn, cucumbers and boxes of peaches. Some for John and the equal number for me. The trailer could handle the load, but it was a struggle for my six-cylinder Meteor station wagon. We came over the Big Ben highway again, everything held together, and we all dined on fresh goodies for a few days. The next summer the Rogers Pass opened up and it seemed that every

94

friend we knew went to British Columbia and had to stop at the Elliott's in Cochrane. It got so bad that Helen finally put her foot down and said, "I'm tired of cooking, washing sheets every morning, and making up the chesterfield every night – we're going on holidays." I wrangled some leave and we went to Radium, BC. to enjoy a quiet holiday.

With the expansion of the City of Calgary and increased rural population law enforcement could not carry on as usual. Our Officer Commanding, whose name I have purposefully left out, was an alcoholic. If he inspected your detachment, he expected you to have a bottle of rye and it would be finished before he left. This did not work for me as I never gave him a drop of liquor and consequently was not his favourite NCO. One of many stupid things he did was set up a two-man highway patrol at the Seebe Calgary Power dam. The only reason for this was free housing and power and it was halfway between Cochrane and Canmore Detachments. There was not another person living there and the only communication was by police radio. With no office or supplies they were working out of my office, but not under my control. It soon gained the title of the "Nice and Sweet Highway Patrol" – the members were Csts. Ron Nice and Al Sweet.

Around this same time, it became obvious that the large number of members working out of Calgary Detachment were spending too much time driving through the city. They began moving members to the surrounding detachments and I picked up a few more men. I now had ten or so members working out of a two-man office, all hours of the night, right next to our living room. Radio communications had improved, which meant more calls coming in and I finally had to insist that the office radio go silent at 10.00 p.m., and all communication be done from the cars. No matter how much I complained to our Officer Commanding about the house and office accommodation, it fell on deaf ears. After all he had been stationed at Fort Vermilion and these accommodations were much better than that. My salvation came one evening when Cst. Sweet called me on the phone. He started relating how some farmer crossing the #1 Highway with his tractor got hit by a car and the tractor smashed into two pieces. "Was anyone killed?" "No." "Then why the hell are you phoning me?" Silence... "The two guys driving the car are the O.C. and the C.O. and they are both drunk out of their minds." Damn, now I don't have one drunken boss to look after – but two. (One being the Officer Commanding all of Alberta and the Commanding Officer of Calgary Sub/Division).

I knew that the media were always monitoring our radios so my first

95

instructions for Cst. Sweet were to maintain radio silence. I then told him to throw those two drunks into the back seat of a police car and get them to hell out of there. The next was to look after the farmer – really well and tell no one the identity of the drunk drivers. Cst. Sweet was onto this already and that is why he phoned me. At that time the 2 I/C. of the Sub/Division was S/Sgt. Jim Baxter, who was a good guy and had at one time been stationed at Cochrane. I phoned him at home and told him "he had a problem" and that I was not going to get stuck with this one. I learned a few new words, but Jim showed up on the scene and took over the investigation. I never heard one word from either officer, in private or otherwise, thanking us for saving their careers or the good reputation of the Force. We kept it out of the press and next spring the Highway Patrol members duly noted that the farmer had a new and much bigger tractor. The O.C. retired to pension the following spring and we got a new O.C. by the name Insp. Joe Vachon. Joe was both an Officer and a gentleman and although we were far apart in rank, we became good friends.

At the time of Insp. Vachon's arrival I was the Master of King Solomon Masonic Lodge and was expected to attend the annual Alberta Grand Lodge meeting being held in Edmonton. Cst. Moller had several years of experience by then and we had other members around to help so I took the day off and went to Edmonton with a carload of other Masons. It was court day and John was running the show when a clandestine message came out that the new Officer Commanding was in route to inspect the detachment. John sent Moses Ear over to tidy up the place and "The Boss" arrived to find an Indian prowling around the office. No problem, it didn't take him long to inspect the office, which shocked him, and then he and Moses walked over to the Village Hall where court was being held. After court he had an interview with Cst. Moller and arranged with Helen to see the living quarters. John was waiting for me when I got home near midnight and his news could not have been better. I was to phone the O.C. first thing in the morning and we were to start looking for new office space. Insp. Vachon phoned me next morning before I was even in the office and the conversation went something like this; "Cpl. Elliott I couldn't sleep last night at the thought of you having to carry the prisoners' piss pot through your wife's living room. You find new quarters and phone me by noon." It was the happiest "Yes sir" I ever said to an officer. We already had a couple of rooms at the back of Graham's Drug store in mind. I phoned him back, and the Identification came out that afternoon to measure the place and take pictures. Next morning Insp. Vachon phoned back with two words – "Start moving." I had been trying for over three years to get my Officer Commanding to do something and this all happened in 48 hours. I got the word Friday, we all got into working clothes on Saturday, moved the office and by Monday the cell was dismantled and from then on we took all our prisoners directly to Calgary. The sign was gone from the old building and mounted over the new office. With a lot of scrubbing, some curtains, a couple of gallons of paint, and with a new carpet we had a third bedroom. Danny got his own room and there was no more stuffing three growing boys into a broom closet. Everyone was happy to stay in the booming Village of Cochrane for a couple more years.

With the expanded office space, I was starting to get additional men under my control and was doing more administration than actual police work. I had four or five men dedicated to Highway Patrol and since I had Justice of the Peace status, I had to sign all their traffic tickets. That took up the first half hour of each morning. I eventually rated a stenographer and found a middle-aged married woman with lots of office experience. In a couple of months, she was onto our systems, had the office tuned up and best of all – no more typing for me. I had more time for mentoring and training young recruits. I tried to guide them, not boss them and for the most part was able to send out two men on most patrols. Mistakes were made and there were fires to be put out but for the most part the men liked working under my command and I always received a high-performance rating.

There was one funny incident that a recruit never forgot and made great fodder for the local ranchers. At that time Eric Harvey was one of the richest men in Alberta and was running Bow Valley ranch east of Cochrane. They shipped yearly steers right from the ranch to Ontario and we had to act as Brand Inspectors as the cattle were going out of province. I did this most of the time as it was a nice half day off. When I got too busy, I sent out a young Cst. who had about two years total service. Unfortunately, he was a city kid and didn't have much knowledge of livestock. I showed him the Harvey brand in the Brand book, what to look for and noted that he didn't have to worry about them shipping any stolen cattle. He sat on the side of the loading chute enjoying himself all afternoon and when the loading was done declared that they all looked legal to him. To which Neil Harvey declared "You've got better eyes than I have because the brand was on the other side." We all had a good laugh, but I still sent him out again the next fall and this time he got it right.

The last couple of years in Cochrane went by fairly fast with no disasters one way or the other. Helen was teaching, the boys were all in school, playing sports and we were just part of the community. Besides teaching, Helen was taking university courses, plus enjoying her annual two weeks of art classes at the Banff School of Fine Arts. During her stay in Banff things sometimes got a little hectic around our house, but I was lucky enough to have a neighbour lady come in and help keep things under control. I sometimes took the boys up on the weekend for a day with "Mum" and one time we tented. We still had time every summer for a family trip to some lake either in British Columbia or northern Saskatchewan. We would tent most of the time and fortunately our little tent had been replaced to a much larger two room affair. It took a couple of hours to set up but was pretty comfortable with a sleeping room and a separate cooking and eating area.

My first November in Cochrane I discovered that there was very little in the way of a proper Armistice celebration. The three major churches did their own thing on a Sunday, not necessarily the same one, and the Legion had their service in the Legion building. The second year I began discussing this matter with all the parties and ended up chairing a committee. That's all it took and soon we had everyone working together and ended with a very nice ecumenical service in the Village Hall. The Anglican, Roman Catholic and United ministers all took part with the Legion members handling the flags together with the Acts of Remembrance. There was a Roman Catholic priest out from Calgary who had a magnificent baritone voice and when he sang the rafters shook. I was in Calgary a few days later and asked my Roman Catholic buddy, Sgt. Mike Collins of the GIS (General Investigation Service) if he happened to know the guy. He looked at me with a grin on his face and said "Ya, I know him – he's my brother." He was also a good friend of Fr. Gandolf who ran the RC Retreat Centre at the top of the Cochrane Hill.

The RC church was right behind the Detachment and a runaway truck missed the church, they hit the RCMP building. The church had a big lawn and Fr. Gandolf would bring his power lawn mower down from the Centre and cut the lawn himself. We got to know each other and soon he was storing his mower in our garage. I got to use it to cut our lawn and also the lawn at the Masonic hall. A hot day of mowing lawns brings on a beer and we were soon sharing a common friendship. This went on for a while and I soon determined that the Priest was not a happy man and seemed to be at odds with the Church and especially the Bishop's autocratic dictates. While all this was going on the Anglican minister David Carter was also commiserating with the good Father and he came to the same conclusion. All this came to an end on an Easter Monday after prayers and the Retreat "broke the fast." He called his staff together and told them he was leaving, no explanation where he

Me and my boys
David   Lee   Danny

was going or anything – just leaving. Before noon on Tuesday I got a call from a farmer telling me that he was driving into town and he was sure he saw Fr. Gandolf hitch-hiking east on No. 1 highway and all he was carrying was a little black satchel. Early next morning the RC Bishop phoned me, and he was not mad - he was ballistic. "What do you know? What did you do? Where is he going?" I told him what the farmer told me – nothing else. The last I heard was that the Good Father had been defrocked and was as happy as a clam running a bar in northern Ontario. David Carter went into politics and ended up as Speaker of the Provincial Legislature. Police work was not boring, but you never knew who your next enemy might be!

When I arrived at Cochrane, I had to learn to hunt in the mountains rather than in the bush. Fortunately, Ray Hill was a forest ranger at the Ghost ranger station with his wife Margaret and two boys about the same age as Danny and David. So, while Margaret and Helen talked about us, the boys played together while Ray and I went about putting food on the table. Over my lifetime of hunting in that area I managed to harvest several elk, a couple of moose, a few deer, together with a mountain goat and a grizzly bear. I considered the bear a trophy and had the hide mounted. The area northwest of Cochrane was also a nice place to snowmobile, and as long as I lived in Calgary it was my favourite place to go as I knew all of the trails and cut lines. It was also a great location for our family to go on our annual Christmas tree outing (we never bought a tree and always cut our own) which I've carried on with my granddaughters. Danny and Lee are still carrying on this tradition with their families.

Police work could present you with some real dilemmas. This happened to Cst. John Moller and I on a Christmas eve early in my Cochrane adventures. We were checking traffic on the TransCanada Highway which was still only a single lane road at that time. We stopped a logging truck heading west only to find it had a second truck winched

Here I am off to put meat on the table

up to the back and there was no safety chain nor any lights on the back truck. That was just a start, as we found both the driver and passenger intoxicated and they turned out to be two well-known brothers from south of Cochrane. They owned and ran a logging business out of Bragg Creek and were both friends and my best contact source for that entire area. Policemen can only be in one place at a time and if you're going to police an area you need contacts that are trustworthy and who you could deal with in full confidentiality. My options were limited. Do I arrest them and burn my contacts, or is there another way? I knew there was a farm field gate up the road from where we stopped so I put the two drunks in the back of the police car, John went ahead and opened the gate and turned his emergency lights on while I drove the truck. Backing up one truck is bad enough but backing up two when they are only connected with the cable is like pushing cooked spaghetti through a pound of frozen butter. I was prepared to give it a try rather than going out in the field and getting stuck. To my total surprise I made it all in one try without even changing

100

gears. I locked up the truck and drove our two friends home with them professing loudly that "I was the best damn truck driver in Alberta." Little did they know that sometimes you can also be lucky - they were and so was I. I had played favouritism - but now I had a stick, and nothing happened in the Bragg Creek area that I didn't hear about.

When I was Master of the King Solomon Masonic Lodge in 1965, I decided to have a formal lady's banquet and dance. This was not received with any great enthusiasm by the men, but it soon caught fire with the ladies, and they were off to buy long gowns, white elbow length gloves, shoes and all the other accoutrements which help keep wives happy. The mayor, councillors, local parliamentarians and businesspeople were invited as guests. That first lady's night was held at Eamon's Restaurant and Lounge on the 1A highway. Tickets were $7.00 a couple, which covered admission, banquet, live orchestra and a corsage for the ladies. The hall was filled to capacity, the evening was a huge success and we turned a tidy profit of $149.95. The Masonic lady's night carried on at various locations in Cochrane and Calgary for 23 years and it took the Calgary Winter Olympics to affect its demise. Our Ladies Night was usually held to coincide with Valentine's Day which was the opening day for the Olympics. Social norms were changing and ballroom dancing which was so popular during and right after WWII was being replaced by clubs, theatre and stay at home TV watchers. Change was obvious by the time we left Cochrane as new businesses were opening up and the beginning of a residential building boom had commenced. People were commuting to Calgary for work and Cochrane was no longer a little cowboy village at the bottom of the Big Hill, but was rapidly switching from a rural to an urban centre.

When I finished my seven years in Cochrane, I was one of the senior Cpls. in all of Alberta. I was past due for a promotion to Sgt., however since Edmonton and Ottawa had never gotten around to combining both the Highway patrol and detachment personnel under one command, I didn't have enough men directly under me to qualify for a promotion. In February 1967 word came that I was being transferred to 3 I/C Calgary Detachment. This was not a position I was happy with but at least we were moving to Calgary and that fit in with our plans as my retirement was looming. Helen would be getting her own house again after living in crappy government accommodation for 10 years and we would be close to a university.

My replacement was my good friend Sgt. Ralph Toews, but the transfer would not take place immediately. Everyone was happy and our first project was either to buy or build a house. We could find no homes that we liked anywhere near the university and soon decided that we would build a place to our own specifications. The salesman that we picked was trying to put us into the Silver Springs area which was still nothing but an open field. I wouldn't buy this so under pressure he finally relented and showed me two lots on the west end of Uxbridge Drive in University Heights. He didn't want to show me these as they were far too expensive at $5,300. That winter you could get into a starter home in Brentwood for $385 combined with a free Government winter works grant of $500. We bought the lot at 2411 Uxbridge Drive, found a builder and started our new home. Helen was ecstatic, while I was wondering if I could pay the $165 a month mortgage and still meet my other bills. Our house was a split level, so we had the builder only finish the top floor. I finished the lower floor myself and eventually added a detached garage. We lived in that house for 19 years until moving to our current condo in Varsity Estates.

Once we got our house plans worked out and a contractor hired our next big adventure was the 67 World Expo in Montreal. We had been planning for some time to do a family trip and with Dave and Jeanie in Ottawa, what better time than to tie these two together. We also had good friends in Montreal, Rev. Gavin Barnett and his wife who had been the Anglican Minister in Fort Vermilion. They now had children of their own and had invited us for a visit as soon as the Exposition in Montreal had been confirmed. Although it was in writing that I was being transferred no date had been set for the move. Ralph Toews had only been in Canmore for three years when he was moved to Calgary for a plainclothes position. He didn't like this type of work and was happy to be getting back to a rural detachment. However, a replacement had to be found for him and the moves were not coordinated and confirmed until August 1, 1967. In the meantime, I had been promoted to Sgt. effective April 1. This was about four years after I had expected it but I knew it was coming eventually. I turned down a Sgt's position in Fort MacLeod as I was not going back to fighting Indians and Helen wanted a move to Calgary. The refusal to move was not actually in writing but with growth we now had two officers in Calgary and the newest Officer was a young Insp. by the name of Irv Blim. We had hunted bighorn sheep and elk together and the difference in rank was no barrier to our friendship. He phoned me at home one night to say that they were throwing darts to see who was being transferred where and that I was slated for Fort MacLeod. He got a quick answer; "Irv if they do that you will have my resignation in the morning."

His answer was, "I thought so" and that was the end of that move.

The building of our house was running behind schedule, which is not unusual, and we were not going to be able to move in until after the September long weekend. This left me in a quandary as Ralph was moving into the barracks a month before that. With consent of the O.C. Ralph agreed that we could store my furniture in the Detachment garage at Cochrane. We lined the garage with plastic and the movers packed up everything except for enough uniforms to last me a week and our holiday clothes for our trip to Montreal. Our friends Ted and Jean Hennig were on holidays, so we camped in their house for that week.

When it became known that we were being transferred and were going on a holiday to Montreal, Gene Fullerton, owner of the Bragg Creek Trading Post, offered me the use of his holiday trailer. He was another one of my contacts. This was a fairly new well-equipped 16-foot single axle trailer and was all we needed. By now I had traded in my 67 Mercury for a Plymouth four-door station wagon with a V-8 engine. This was perfect for our needs as we had lots of room both in the station wagon and the trailer itself.

I had 21 days holiday and with the two weekends our trip to Montreal covered just about a whole month. We left on a Friday night and got as far as Bassano on the shakedown run. Our next day was to Regina where we toured the RCMP Depot Division. The following day we were in Winnipeg where we visited Fort Garry and the boys got to see their first stone fort and what it was like when the Hudson's Bay arrived. It took three days to drive across northern Ontario to Ottawa with nothing much to see but "Watch for Moose" signs. We did see Cochrane, Ontario where my mail frequently ended up and also the high point of land where the water flowed into both the Atlantic and Arctic oceans. Ottawa had grown somewhat in the twenty years since I had left training, but I found Dave and Jeanie's place with no problem. We stayed with them for about a week and Jeanie showed us the city including the Mint, Parliament buildings, War Memorial and all the other must-see things in our nation's capital. Dave took us on a drive into the Gatineau hills of Quebec. The road was very scenic but twisty and the kids enjoyed the ride more than Helen. It was another day's drive to Montreal, and we were happy to be united with the Barnett's again and see their children. We visited the expo for about five days which was a lot of walking and standing in line. Danny and Dave got a ride across the river on a hydrofoil, but Lee was too young to go, much to his disappointment. We came back to Ottawa, left the boys with Dave and Jeanie while Helen and I took a two-day trip

Our home away from home to Montreal and back

to Halifax to visit Aunt Louise.

Coming back, we went through the northern United States and it was a much quicker trip. It was a wonderful and memorable trip with only one slight misadventure and that was when I changed my pants to go out for dinner and left the trailer key locked in the trailer. Fortunately, there was a storage space under the rear bed which was accessible from the outside. With the car jack I was able to lift the bed up high enough to "stuff Lee" through and recover our keys. Helen looked after the keys from then on. On our last day somewhere around Brooks, Helen and I were smiling over the conversations in the backseat. Then Danny announced in a very proud voice "See Dad, I told you we could go all the way and back without having a fight – and we did." Our boys were boys but BOTH parents thought they were the best in the world – and I still do.

Calgary

Our house was still not finished to move into on September 1, so the builder put us up in a motel for a couple of days. On Tuesday after the long weekend we finally took possession of our house and our household goods were moved in from Cochrane on Wednesday. It was hectic getting our stuff moved in and organized and at the same time settling our kids into three different schools. Helen was busy with that while I was getting myself orientated into my new job. I had been my own boss for 10 years and it was a little different with someone else calling the shots. It was a busy time but also exciting especially for Helen, she could get back to her decorating, hanging pictures and turning a house into a home. The boys were settling into school, making new friends and we found a new place to worship at St. Andrews Anglican church. St. Andrews also had a very active scout troop and the four of us "boys" were soon active again in scouting. Making new friends came easily and after a few months we found ourselves fully immersed into city life. Fortunately, there was no crime to involve you at Sub/Division as all of the real police work was being handled by the rural detachments surrounding the city.

I thought the move had gone off without a hitch until the next spring when I found myself missing a very expensive bamboo fly rod and case. When I was stationed in High Prairie, I stayed in the High Prairie Hotel. An American senior travelling alone to Alaska died in his sleep as a result of a heart attack. Of course, I was the first one there after the cleaning lady found him dead in his bed. We had to trace down and notify his next of kin who requested that the body be sent back to the US. All this was arranged but we still had the car and all his possessions to look after for several months. Among his possessions was a fancy wood custom case with a bamboo fly rod with three different weight tips. This was obviously a very expensive fly rod and I doubt if it had ever been used. When the son came to pick up the car, he said no one in the family had any use whatsoever for this fly rod and gave it to me for having looked after his father's body and property. It was obvious that one of the movers had stolen my fly rod during one of the moves. One set of movers moved our furniture from the house into the garage and another moved it to Calgary a month later. I took the theft up with the moving company but of course they denied everything and there was no way I could take any action against them. I was not much for fly fishing anyway, so it was no great loss, but I was a little annoyed at myself for letting it happen. When you are moving a whole houseful of furnishings a small item or two can disappear very easily.

Stationed on Calgary Detachment was a huge step backwards as far as I was concerned. S/Sgt. Peter Pailey was in charge, followed by Sgt. Doug Simmons and I was the third man. This meant that I was the "gopher" and got stuck with all the odd jobs and I was also back on shift duty. As a result, I sometimes had to work evenings and weekends. One of my more frequent and less desirable tasks was to notify next of kin, usually on the death of their husband, some relative or worst of all that their son or daughter would not be coming home as a result of a motor vehicle accident. This was always stressful, never pleasant but I seemed to be well suited for the job. I usually tried to contact a neighbour to get information on the person, see if a friend or even a priest was available, but most of the time you just knocked on the door and broke the news. This invariably resulted in shock, screaming, tears and quite often the only thing I could do was hold them and hug them until they got themselves under control. Not an ideal job for a policeman with 20 years of service who had witnessed too many fatal accidents. There is only one death I remember with real clarity and that was a woman in Forest Lawn. Her husband had been killed in a trucking accident. I contacted the neighbour who informed me "Oh she's going to go into shock... she's going to faint... she's going to do everything else. You should have a doctor present." I knocked on the door, broke the news and her reply was "It's about time the son of a bitch got it." As I said before, police work can be both exciting and boring, but you never knew when the next surprise was going to hit you.

The Calgary Sub/Division had a social club which looked after things like transfers in and transfers out, promotions etc. and I gravitated towards that to play on my strengths. Insp. Blim being the junior officer was in charge of the social activities, so we got along just fine. The Sub/Division held a regimental ball every spring and it wasn't long before I was doing most of the organization all the way up to being the emcee. These were sometimes held in the Palliser Hotel but later we switched over to the Calgary Inn on 4th Street. These colourful regimental balls were always very popular, and we usually had 300 to 400 in attendance. As usual we had a politician or two from both the city and province as well as members of the Calgary City Police and the military units which were more prominent in Calgary than today. You could also rest assured that there would be a diplomat from someplace looking for a seat at the head table. With no lengthy criminal cases to tie me up I enjoyed working on some fairly complicated social arrangements.

In addition to the annual regimental ball we had a fall barbecue. This started out as a corn boil at Colpitts barbecue site, which was on the Elbow River south of Spring Bank. Since there were just a few old tables in the bush along the riverbank I soon moved our venue to the Tecumseh Naval Museum at 17th and 24th street in Calgary. After a couple of commercial failures S/Sgt. Gus Buziak from Calgary GIS and myself took over the barbecue and did our own cooking. We became quite a team, built up a reputation for good food and good fun, carrying on this tradition for several years after we had both retired. Gus was the chief chef and supervised the cooking with the help of many others and I looked after the organization and the ticket sales. We barbecued the old way with briquettes which started about six in the morning and we would put on anywhere between 200 and 300 pounds of standing rib roasts for the banquet at 7 PM. Cooking the gallons of beans modified with secret ingredients was our biggest problem. They had to be cooked at the very lowest speed all day or would burn, and unless you stood over them with a cleaver in hand some energetic know-it-all would come along and turn up the heat. Beef, corn on the cob, butter and buns usually completed the meal which was followed by a dance with live orchestra. We carried on this tradition for a number of years but stopped for a hiatus as we were going our separate ways. Gus and I got together again a few years ago to cook barbecues for the RCMP VETS which was a much smaller group. We cooked our last barbecue about 10 years ago. We got to be popular enough that the Blood Indians wanted us to help them barbecue two Buffalo for a powwow. We were smart enough to graciously decline their request.

In early 1969 there was another change in my status which was not of my own making or what I would've chosen as a career. On 23 December Sgt. Sandy Sondergaard was returning from Brooks when he went into the ditch and hit a power pole. Unfortunately, he hit it about 20 feet up, the car landed on its roof and by the time he sobered up in hospital I was the Calgary Sub/Division Traffic NCO It was called a Force transfer - positions switched at no cost. I was now my own boss; I had my own office but no staff. My job was to coordinate traffic enforcement from the British Columbian Border, north past Crossfield and south to Nanton and east to Brooks.

Being transferred to Highway coordinator in the middle of winter had certain advantages as I had time to figure out what my job was before the busy summer driving season. I had my own office and car but there was no manual covering my position and I was never one for writing traffic tickets. I had forty-four men at nine detachments to lead and my first job was to visit all of these units and find out from them how we could improve our joint efforts. I also had to establish good relationships with the detachment commanders as they were overseers of all members, both detachment and Highway Patrol. I soon found that their complaints were all the same, we needed better high-speed equipment and more unmarked cars. The cars we had were fast enough but better tires, lights and safety equipment that was available were not being supplied. I am sure that in my three years on highway patrol I wrote more reports on this topic than all others put together. I didn't have much success during my term as Traffic Coordinator but many of my suggestions eventually came to fruition.

In the 1970s there were no private registration centres like today, and everything was directly under the control of the Provincial Department of Highways. Calgary had the second biggest office in Alberta, and it was under the supervision of Ed Simpson. He was a Navy Veteran, a staunch member of the Naval Veterans Association and a great friend of the RCMP. He was also in charge of a small group of provincial traffic inspectors who basically ran the weigh scales and checked truck traffic. We ended up collaborating on many joint traffic check stops where all traffic was directed through the weigh scales. They looked after the trucks and we checked everyone for driver's license and insurance. I would call in the Highway Patrol from surrounding Detachments and with our two enforcement agencies we would have at least forty traffic officers checking everything that moved. We picked up the odd drunk driver but for the most part it was suspended drivers, driver's license expired, no driver's license or no insurance. The provincial officers' big haul was usually equipment deficiencies and improper licensing. It seldom took too long before we had a yard full of parked trucks. On a smaller scale our two enforcement units ran a free holiday trailer inspection each spring. With volunteers from the trailer salespeople, propane dealers and mechanics you could have your trailer weighed, including hitch weight, lights, propane and brakes checked and minor adjustments made if possible. All these trailer checks were made at the Balzac weigh scales. It got so popular that we had trailers lined up back to the city limits and we had to discontinue this free service after two years. It was a good PR move and showed the other side of traffic policemen.

Before I could get into too much traffic coordination, I had to take a course on radar operations and also aircraft traffic observer. Both of these courses were taught internally and after a year or so I ended up doing the instructions on both. A certificate of proficiency was needed to testify in court on these matters. The aircraft traffic enforcement had been tested in Edmonton and was in operation there before Calgary. I set up all operations in Calgary which meant measuring the markers on the various highways. This was done with a department of highways engineer and one of our members so that we could testify in court as to the accuracy of the highway measurements. I did some of this myself before getting the members out and letting them know what it was like on the end of a 300-foot survey chain.

The aircraft used in our enforcement were rented and this led to contracts with the Calgary Flying Club. Since I was the only qualified observer I got in a lot of flying time, which led to me obtaining a private pilot's license. Danny had also acquired a pilot's license and together we bought a used B12 Taylor-craft, CF-DOK. This was a side-by-side tail dragger with no electronics. You started the engine by spinning the prop and hoping you had it well tied down or somebody in the pilot seat. It was a fun little airplane to fly but expensive to maintain and we soon found somebody we disliked and sold it to him. Danny had an interest in a Citabria aircraft and took me up for a ride one day. I continued with my private pilot's license until 1977 when I finally gave it up. By that time, I was certified to fly on five different aircraft and had a fair number of hours. By then I was working for the Royal Bank of Canada (RBC) and had lost all interest in flying. I was also a director of the Calgary Flying Club for over 10 years.

Back to Highway Patrol – Ed Simpson and I spent many hours discussing traffic problems, speed limits, highway markings and in general working together to improve driving conditions. I can't claim credit for any one thing in particular, but during my watch we did synchronize car and truck speed limits. At that time trucks had a slower speed limit than cars. We also got the passing lanes implemented. Surprisingly the first passing lanes in use were not under Alberta control but were at Lake Louise which is a federal government highway. The aircraft patrol was basically restricted to summer as the markings were often snow-covered for several months during the winter. In my second year I got a designated aircraft patrol observer. He was young Cst. by the name of Alan Palmer. He is now retired in Cochrane and a member of the Calgary vets but I seldom see him.

During my patrol as traffic coordinator I had many serious accidents but was never first on the scene. We had four multiple death level railway crossing accidents which were particularly disturbing as three of them wiped out entire families. One in particular comes to mind because of the miracle survival of one of the passengers. It was near High River where the railway track runs from the south east to the northwest and the highway directly north/south. Early in the morning a car was driving south and obviously at a very high rate of speed. There were no signs of skid marks whatsoever. The car hit the right front corner of the first train engine and just exploded. The car engine was out of the frame with parts and debris scattered over a wide area. The driver was killed, while his wife and son were in vegetative states. When the engineer got his train stopped about three quarters of a mile down the track, he heard a baby crying in the right ditch. He could not get out the right door so he had to get out the left side. When he ran around he found and picked up a baby girl who had been stuck on the side of the engine until the train jerked to a stop. She was not hurt, and her total injuries were covered by a band aid on one finger. How she went through the car windshield and all the debris at 100 miles an hour, then stuck on the side of the train engine until it jerked to a stop is an absolute miracle.

Another remarkable survival accident happened on the bridge over the Waiparous River on No. 40 highway northwest of Cochrane. Four oil workers were going out for the night shift in a four-door truck. The bridge over the Waiparous River was on an 'S' curve and the deck was covered with loose gravel. Unfortunately, they were going too fast and slammed into the side of the bridge. The bridge was an old metal one with lots of small metal beams. An inch and a half piece of angle iron came loose, went through the right rear door, the right rear passenger, through the back of the truck and into a gas tank in the truck box. No vital organs in the passenger were hit, but when the first ambulance arrived, they could do little more than take care of his pain. A Calgary fire truck was next on the scene to cut the metal but all they had was a chop saw which made sparks so with the gas leaking they were likewise of no help. A second fire truck arrived, and the man was finally cut free with a three foot long piece of angle iron still stuck through his body. It was a slow and gentle ride to the Foothills Hospital where they arrived about 8:00 a.m. and the surgery team was waiting. Five weeks later that same passenger walked into the RCMP office at Cochrane, as healthy and happy as could be, wanting some pictures of his accident. I don't know whether or not he framed them with the piece of metal from his accident, but he was one lucky oil worker. I wrote these two incidents up for the annual national traffic report but never saw them published. Working in the Mounted Police in my time was often routine, but when you went to work you never knew what the shift might bring.

I started my traffic duties in early 1969 and by the time spring arrived in 1972 it was a well-known fact I was fed up with traffic, stuck in a Sgt. position and was looking for a change. Because of my extensive work in the Sub/Division recreational field I was on good working terms with the O.C. Supt. Peter Wright. He assured me that a change was coming, and it did, but not until July. We were still having the annual Sub/Division banquet in the spring and Gus Buziak and I were still running the fall barbecue. However, since the traffic members were scattered all over southern Alberta, we had never had a party or gathering just for us. With my assurance that the detachment members would cover for us, Peter Wright let me host a Highway Patrol party at our house in Calgary. Not all the members could make it, nevertheless, it was a good bonding party. In the 10 days or so before the function Cst. Palmer was out shopping quite often, and I even gave him hell for not doing any work. I had to eat some of those words in a presentation at the party. We were presented with a beautiful silver tray bearing the following inscription:

ROYAL CANADIAN MOUNTED POLICE
to
SGT. and Mrs. A.G. (Curly) ELLIOTT
In APPRECIATION
CALGARY SUB.DIVISION HIGHWAY PATROLS

It is one of my most cherished RCMP items as it was strictly voluntarily given, and it justly included Helen.

I was transferred to I/C. Calgary Detachment and promoted to Staff /Sergeant

(S/Sgt.) on July 20, 1972. Supt. Peter Wright in his Recommendation for Promotion wrote the following and I finally got an acknowledgment that I could fully agree with.

This Senior NCO has considerable General Duty experience and will have no difficulty at his new post. He is a versatile member who was converted from General Duty to Sub-Division Traffic NCO at Force request in early 1969 and did a good job but favours the General duty field. He is very strong on public relations and shows good leadership ability. Sgt. Elliott is also a strong supporter of the Sub-Division in the recreational field and is noted for his forthright opinion and honesty. He has been well reported on and this recommendation is made without reservation.

Calgary Detachment was almost all administrative. I had both a Sgt. and a Cpl. under my command. We had very little crime to worry about, as that was all handled by the G.I.S. plain clothes members. We had no rural area to police as that was all covered by the surrounding detachments. We still had a guardroom, a court detail and the office was open on a 24/7 basis, which meant judicious scheduling of your manpower. There was no paid overtime and I worked longer hours than most and had a very cohesive staff.

The RCMP was officially established by an Order in Council signed by Prime Minister John A. MacDonald on May 23rd, 1873. With the 100th anniversary approaching the Sub/Division Social Club decided to do something special. Instead of the usual spring banquet and ball in Calgary we would move it to the Banff Springs Hotel in Banff. I was elected as committee chairman and TOLD that I would also be the emcee. The hotel was then owned by the CP Rail, with whom we had a long-standing relationship. We started negotiating with the hotel at least four years before the actual event to secure space and set prices. Our original target was for 500 attendees but in the end, we went over 700 which meant overflows to other hotels. Supt. Peter Wright was still the O.C. and had the final say but largely left the organizing up to me and my conscripted co-chair S/Sgt. Jack (Helen) Patterson. We made many trips to Banff and a few to Edmonton as all of "K" Division was now involved, Things didn't get really hectic until the last six months and by then we had plans for a three-day fun weekend and even planned programs for kids.

Arrivals started early Friday afternoon and that night we had an outdoor western barbecue provided by the Banff Springs Hotel. To add some fun and a western flair we even made up a little MP branding iron and painted it red. Dipped in a fire of dry ice it came out smoking and any stray heifer caught had it applied to her right hip. This got off to a slow start but after a few rounds of libations we had a whole herd of gals branded up. Our only mishap occurred at that barbecue when some visiting member tripped and stuck his hand into the hot coals of a big fire pit. He was rushed off to hospital and showed up at the banquet and ball with a hand totally wrapped in bandages, however that didn't dampen his spirit and he enjoyed the weekend as much as anyone else. I expect his hand was sore for a while and his typing greatly restricted. David, Lee and Bruce Armstrong were together in a separate hotel and since David had just gotten his driver's license, they enjoyed their grown-up weekend doing their own thing. Jack Patterson and I with the help of some Banff members and a lot of hotel staff had spent two days decorating the main ballroom with flags, RCMP hundred anniversary posters and other memorabilia. The backdrop for the head table was several sheets of white Styrofoam painted with welcoming remarks and comments celebrating our 100-year anniversary.

The head table was my biggest problem as it grew to a total of twenty-four. We had everybody from Commr. William Higget to the youngest Cst. in the subdivision. The junior Cst. in true military fashion gave the toast to the queen. We had the C.O. "K" Division and our own Supt. Peter Wright, but also every diplomat, politician and VIP who had managed to secure a ticket. Naturally all of them wanted to be seen at the head table. As was the custom at that time we arranged male and female seating and had name place cards for everyone. The American ambassador's wife screwed this all up when around 4:00 o'clock she decided she was too sick to attend. I was not about to start changing things at that time and we just took her plate and card off and left it be. There was not a single RCMP serving member in Alberta at that time who played the bagpipe, so I ended up with my good friend Bill Campbell from the Calgary City Police as my piper. There was the usual receiving line which was far too long so when the time arrived, I had Bill fire up his pipes and the head table was piped in. Every table and chair in the hotel were pressed into use and we had people in the doorways filling every nook and cranny. The first hiccup occurred when I told people to be seated. The hotel had set twenty-four places at the table but there were only twenty-two chairs. Even with the American ambassador's wife missing, I had no place to sit. This was soon rectified by a chair from the lounge but while the rest got soft chairs, I as usual got the hard chair. Poor me!

I was able to keep all of the speakers to their allotted time and by 9:00 o'clock we were ready to leave the banquet room and move to the Grand Ballroom.

Because of the crowded banquet room one of the hotel staff moved Bill Campbell's pipes and set them on a heat register – a real no-no! The bag dried out and when Bill went to pipe us into the ballroom it was like blowing into a sieve. That cost me a couple of extra scotches. However, being a true Scot, he persevered and got us into rows of sixteen, led by the three senior officers. We had a twelve-piece band and the festivities carried on well into Sunday morning. Professional photographers were on hand, old friends reunited, and new ones made. As usual groups returned to their rooms and I am sure the sun was up before the last story was told. Helen and I had a huge suite on the sixth floor with lots of flowers, fruit and a few bottles of wine supplied. Helen entertained Ted and Jean Hennig, Dave and Jeanie Armstrong and I seem to remember a few others crowded in while I delivered banquet flowers to deserving rooms.

Not too many were down for breakfast which was not included in the ticket price and we finished the event off with a short ecumenical church service. Everyone went home happy, raving about what a wonderful centennial celebration weekend and accolades flowed like water. We came in under budget and the Banff Springs Hotel was most pleased with our cooperative working together, welcoming us back any time. Jack Patterson and all our committee members were thanked for all our time and efforts with the greatest praise coming from the host Supt. Peter Wright. This party was raved about for years, as were some of my comments made at the head table. I had a habit of singling out Commrs. for some of my one-liners and not thinking through the consequences. However, I didn't worry too much as by then I knew I was going to retire in six months and was already looking for a new job.

About the same time as we were celebrating in Banff the first world oil crisis was coming into full bloom and airports everywhere were scrambling to increase their security. Canada was no exception and the RCMP was frantically recruiting Special Csts. specifically for airport duty. Most of these recruits had some military experience, got a short six weeks training course in Regina, were issued a plain brown serge uniform with Special Constable Shoulder flashes and sent out to airports across Canada.

Calgary Sub/Division had a detachment at the airport, but it only consisted of a Corporal, two Constables and nineteen Commissionaires. This was going to be greatly increased and one day when Peter Wright and I were returning from a centennial organizational meeting he turned to me and said, "Who are we going to send to the airport?" I looked at him and said, "What about Curly Elliott?" He gave me a shocked look and said, "You wouldn't go." To which I replied, "Ask me and see." Two days later I was transferred from Calgary Detachment to Calgary International Airport detail. It was the beginning of my most interesting posting.

I mentioned staying under part three of the RCMP pension plan, which was to my advantage when it came time to retire as my pension was based on my last 12 months of service. Under part five the pension plan was based on your best five years. When I got promoted to S/Sgt., I knew that this the highest rank I would ever obtain, and I started making plans to retire when I had in my one full year of service. Helen and I started making retirement travelling plans and I was wondering what my future employment would be. I had to keep it all a secret as I already had several job offers, but was not too interested in most of them. A new RCMP retiree named Bill Carter from Regina came to Calgary to work for the CIBC as security for some new card payment system called Chargex. Not too long after that a Royal Bank advertisement appeared in the local paper looking for someone to fill a similar position for them. I talked to Bill to see what it was all about and submitted my application for the job. I was interviewed by Jack Duggan, head of Western Canada Visa security for RBC and I got the job. My starting pay was $15,000 per year plus a car and all bank benefits, which was more than I was making after 25 years in the RCMP.

Helen was teaching full-time and we had long planned on making a European trip. If this was going to happen, it had to be in August. This meant more planning and when we had things more or less figured out, I walked into Peter Wright's office and told him why I had taken the transfer to the airport. He had already figured out that I was likely planning on retirement and his only question was how much I was getting paid. When I told him, he was pleased and wished me well in my new career.

I still had a few hectic months before me and my first task was setting up the airport detail. The airport was operating under a rather convoluted agreement between the City of Calgary and the federal government. The City of Calgary controlled the physical structures and federal aviation department, the flying part of the airport. The man who ran the Calgary operation was the most uncooperative person I ever worked with. I was not the first one to lock horns with him as he was also the head of the Calgary Stampede Board. Tom Hall, the late husband of my current partner, Norreen, was VP of the Stampede Board and this man was so miserable with the staff that one employee even committed suicide because of him.

That was not going to happen on my watch. We only had a three-person office at the airport, and I had new Special Csts. coming in almost daily. I ended up with my two NCO's, forty-four special Csts. and I still had nineteen commissaries to look after. I took over a cubbyhole of an office which was all right for a Cpl. and two Csts., but it was no good for three NCO's, plus all the Specials. There was one desk and one telephone, and my first job was to find some more office space. That's where the person running the operation and I locked horns right off the bat and he was impossible to deal with. I turned him over to the Sub/Division, suggesting that if they didn't get better results than I did we should go directly to Ottawa and take the back-door route. After about a month we finally got a slightly larger room and I was able to borrow furnishings from the Sub/Division. I still had no secretary and was too busy to type myself, so I turned that over to the Cpl. My next job was writing up a manual to cover not only my position and the other two NCO's but for all the special Csts. coming in. That was followed by a time sheet covering 24/7 which was impossible when I had more members arriving every week. I soon realized that there was no security on the airport and that was confirmed with my first emergency which was a cow and calf moose wandering on the active runway with an aircraft fast approaching to land. My good friend and neighbour Brian Montgomery was in the business of renting helicopters at the airport at that time and I talked him into a sightseeing tour around the perimeter. To our surprise we found several places where there was no fencing whatsoever. If the coulees were too steep or the bush too thick, they just left it. On top of that there was an open gate for the pizza delivery to bring food to the control tower at all hours of the day and night. Lack of security was multiplied by the gas trucks having to have an open fence so they could turn their semi-trailers around when servicing aircraft. To top this off we had the Queen coming to town.

At this time the main terminal was located on the south west corner of the airport which had been the original McCall Field in WWII. To appease and honour the Natives a parcel of land to the east of the terminal had been declared an Indian Reserve where the Natives could set up their Teepees in preparation for the Queen's visit. The Queen was coming for a 10-day visit in May to coincide with the hundredth anniversary of the Force. When the Queen's protection services together with the RCMP protection services from Ottawa showed up, my issues with the man who ran the operation were put on the back burner and things started to progress in my favour. As I was in charge of airport security, I got to attend most of the meetings and was truly involved in the preparations. With my workplace rivalry out of the way I was accepted and welcomed by the managers who were actually operating the airport. The office was still in shambles and my biggest job seemed to be welcoming new Specials every day or so. Thank God for my two excellent support NCO's. Passenger and baggage screening were pretty much nonexistent in 1973 and there was no national policy forthcoming covering all affected airports. I perceived our biggest threat was the fact that all international flights left from the loading dock nearest the open gates at the aviation fuel terminals. Anyone could walk off the street, across the tarmac, up the service stairs and onto an international flight. Phoney ID cards could be easily replicated, and no one checked them anyway. Visual surveillance of ground crew and boarding passengers was about all we could do, but that was sufficient to let the public know "The Police are watching." Air Canada pilots gave us some problems as they would leave their hats, jackets and sometimes flight bags sitting unguarded while they went for lunch. Any smart terrorist could have changed himself into a flight member and gone anywhere he wanted. When they ignored our suggestions that this was not a good idea, the matter was rectified by a few of the unattended bags being brought to my office. They soon got the message and like every other airport employee realized that security was everyone's problem.

With the Queen's arrival approaching the airport and all facilities were being spruced up and we received boxes of Union Jack flags together with enough red carpet to cover a tennis court. We put flags on every pole, stick and building we could find and still had lots left over. I don't know how many I ended up with, but I still have at least one in my flag box.

When the Queen and Prince Philip finally arrived, their plane was isolated on the tarmac and immediately surrounded by security services. When the Queen stepped onto the carpet, I took the salute. While the Queen was meeting with the dignitaries, I thought the press were crowding in too close and pushed them back, (there was a 20 foot no-go limit) which got my picture on the front cover of TIME magazine. As soon as the royal party finished the welcoming ceremony, I led them across the airport to the Indian village. The Queen did her walk about, gave a speech, exchanged gifts with the Native elders and was back standing in her open car right on schedule - looking around for Prince Phillip. About then my radio went off "Where the hell is Phillip?" I didn't know where he was as I was looking after the Queen. He was soon located and hurried back to join his wife and the Royal cavalcade headed for the Palliser Hotel. It turned out that Phillip had gotten down on his hands and knees, crawled into a teepee and spent the whole time talking to a squaw. When the Royal party were leaving at the end of their ten day stay, we all met in the VIP lounge at the airport. Small gifts were exchanged, and the security details were thanked for their due diligence. Supt. Peter Wright could not let their arrival at the Indian village go unacknowledged and apologized to Her Majesty for losing her husband to the Indians before she had been in Canada for half an hour. This brought the biggest smile to the Queen's face that we'd ever seen and a twinkle in her eye as she looked over at Phillip. Everyone in the room interpreted her look the same way – "They should have kept him." The Queen visited the Stampede several times during her 10-day visit and Lee got to shake her hand on one of her walkabouts - which was closer to the Queen than I got. RCMP family members got grandstand seats immediately surrounding the Queen, but not me as I was too busy with other security matters.

The last few months in the Force were hectic to say the least. There was always some VIP or head of state arriving at the airport and I was busy preparing for my new job and for our first big trip abroad. The most stressful time at the airport with foreign visitors was the departure from Canada of Indira Gandhi, who was the Prime Minister of India. She had been touring Canada for some time and made her departure from YYC. I was not expecting any trouble until East Indians started arriving at the airport by the busload. We had the west gate onto the runway close guarded and all was going well until her security detail announced that her limo was too long to go over the curb at the west gate and they were going to use the south entrance. That gate was always locked so I had to grab one of the airport managers, jump into my car and race over to get the gate open just as the cavalcade arrived. This left the original gate guarded by a half-dozen special Csts. facing off against several thousand East Indians who are trying to scale or break down the fence. I got back in time with reinforcements, but I was happy to see the tail end of that particular aircraft. I was one of the security details who received the gift of a silk tie from Mrs. Gandhi. Whenever I received any comments on it, I was prone to say "It's a gift from some nice lady leader who got murdered by her own people." Which was true.

On Thursday July 19th, 1973 (according to Helen's records) we left on a one-month tour of Europe, which was the start of 36 wonderful years of worldly travel adventures. We arrived in London at 9 AM on the 20th, rented a car from Self Drive

Helen at Stonehenge

Hire Co. for two weeks for the princely sum of £47.79. Next day we headed south to Brighton, Southampton and then west to Stonehenge and Salisbury Cathedral. At that time, you just parked your car, walked across the grass and rubbed shoulders with those monolithic monsters. I was in absolute awe as to how those hundred-ton stones could be dragged for miles, shaped and set up by human hands. I thought I'd seen the greatest wonder of the world until we arrived at Salisbury Cathedral. How could stones be cut so perfectly and fitted together to build columns 10 feet across and 100's of feet high, supporting stone arches, windows, intricate rooflines and a steeple that reached into the heavens? History in stone continued for the next month and I developed a whole new appreciation of my love of "The mysteries of Masonry and its teachings." Before we left, Helen had been studying art and ancient cathedrals and I was positive this was going to be nothing but an ABC tour - "Another Bloody Cathedral." It was me that could not get enough of them and I was reluctant to leave and move onto the next.

We went through the lake country to Chester where Helen met up with Sandy Boyd, one of her teachers from Silver Springs School who showed us around including Caernarvon Castle in Wales. From there I filled my one wish by making it to Scotland and going to Bridge-O-Calley in Perthshire and finding the very house that Grandpa and Gramma Keay lived in before they came to Canada. We ended our driving trip at a B&B in London where a kid from the car rental picked up the car and the next day, we joined a Cooks Tour for a two-week eight country tour of Europe. Our love for travelling continued until Helen was no longer able to make any strenuous trips and together, we managed five continents and about seventy countries.

When we got back to Calgary towards the end of August my first task was to turn the Airport Security Detail over to some other S/Sgt. After 43 years I don't remember his name, but I was glad to be done with the other guy. By then we had the full complement of forty-four special Csts., and we were still supervising the nineteen commissionaires. I also had to start turning in my kit which involved not only my revolver, ammunition and handcuffs, but also most of my uniforms. After condemning kit for 25 years I had more than I knew what to do with anyway. I had so many complete sets of uniforms that I gave some to Fort Calgary and a complete Red Serge outfit to the museum in Windermere, BC. I still have a few things left in my trunk downstairs and that is going to be for someone else to clean out.

With the loss of total government care I had to start learning how to live as a civilian. No more DVA doctors or dentists no matter how terrible they may have been. Besides finding new medical services I now had to arrange for health insurance for all the family, not to mention buying more clothes if I was going to look like a banker. I still had holidays left so I had lots of spare time to make the changeover and my discharge certificate shows that I was in the Force from August 30, 1947 to September 30, 1973, a total of 26 years and 32 days. That was long enough. I made it to the rank of S/Sgt. which was the highest non- commissioned officer rank and I had fulfilled my childhood dream of being "A Mountie."

A few years before I retired, we graduated from the tenting era and I had a 3/4-ton Chevy truck with a nine-foot custom made camper. We had some nice holidays in that but again decided that it was not the ultimate solution and we started looking for lake side property in British Columbia. In 1971 Danny was working in the Yukon for Fred Welter so Dave and Lee joined their parents for a summer cottage lot hunting holiday through the Eastern mountain lakes of BC. We checked out Windermere, Wasa, Christina, Kootenay and Arrow Lakes before crossing over the Monashee Mountains into the Okanagan Valley. On the second last day of our trip we found what we were looking for at Two Mile sub/division just south of Sicamous. We contacted the sales agent in Salmon Arm who came over the next morning, we negotiated an offer, gave him a cheque and headed home to Calgary. We were still unpacking the camper when the phone rang, and we had our lot. We spent the next few years clearing trees and the neighbour's trash off the lot before we could build. The lots on both sides were already developed and they had thrown their bush over onto ours. We also had some large hemlock trees to fell and saw into firewood. Two of them were in the front ditch, our lot was 135 feet deep and when our neighbour Jack Mitchell felled them for us, they reached thirty feet into the undeveloped lot behind us. We cut them into fireplace blocks, split and piled them, giving us firewood for several years.

It was 1977 by the time we got the lot cleared, our cottage plans drawn up by an architect and found the right contractor to build our dream retirement home. Even then the builder didn't follow the plans. He put the centre roof beam in the wrong place and made our cottage a foot higher than it should have been. Fortunately, Helen was a tree hugger so we had lots of trees left and it didn't look too much like a prairie grain elevator. None of the inside of the building was finished and it took me several summers before the inside and fireplace were fully completed. We had no carpets in the living room and Helen had painted the floor three different colours before the carpet was finally laid. That first Thanksgiving Jeanie, Dave and Bruce came up from Vancouver and Jean and Ted Hennig came out from Calgary. Jean brought her piano accordion, Ted his drums and Dave a guitar.

Helen and her dad on the deck

We invited some of the neighbours and christened our little cottage with a real fun party. For 27 years Helen and I enjoyed our summers and the odd Christmas at "The Cottage." We golfed, boated, skied winter and summer, tubed, fished, quadded, dirt biked and snowmobiled in the mountains and enjoyed the company of family and friends from all over the world. I built a garage/workshop and drove Helen crazy with the noise of my wood lathe turning stumps into bowls. However, she usually forgave me when she saw the finished products and especially when I made miniature mushrooms and spinning tops for my little granddaughters. As we aged the cottage became too much for me to keep up and the boys with their own growing families were finding other places to spend their vacations. To avoid capital gains, we turned the cottage over to the three boys several years before it was sold. In 2005 the cottage was sold to a rich farmer from Alberta and the kids got their inheritance early. Those years at the lake and with our ability for worldly travelling were the best and happiest years of our lives.

Preparing the lot - 1975

Helen was busy with her schoolwork and me with my crime-fighting, but we did try to spend as much time together as possible. One of our pleasant twists in life came when a school secretary, Frances Green, convinced Helen that square dancing was a lot of fun and we would both enjoy it. I am not a dancer by any means but was ready to give it a try and we signed up with the Banff Trailers Square Dance Club for beginner's lessons in about 1972. We found that it was in fact a lot of fun, good exercise with a lot of friendship and by graduation the next spring we were hooked. We followed up the square dancing with Round Dancing lessons and this was our main entertainment and exercise for the next 30 years. Square dancing is done with four couples to a caller's instructions, while Round Dancing is done with your partner to choreographed movements which have to be committed to memory. Whenever Helen and I joined any association we never got to sit on the sidelines for very long and so were on the Square Dance executive team in no time. We did our turn as club presidents and later joined the Calgary and District Square and Round Dance Association and were the Social conveners for several years. This Group sponsored a Canadian national square and round dance convention in 1986. We had hundreds of dancers here from all over the world and worked our butts off to ensure that everyone had a good time. There was a colour parade down Stephens Avenue and since Helen and I drew Australia, we led the parade. My last bit of assistance to our club was writing up our Club history, which I did in rhyme, naming every presidential couple, in order, over a 44 year period. We quit dancing when we got older, were travelling a lot and medical problems started slowing us down. By then Square and Round Dancing had tapered off greatly and all clubs were down to just a few squares. Like many other social clubs mixed dancing has been swept into the dust pans of history, socializing of any sort has been lost and replaced by a computer in your pocket.

Another of my interests which Helen and I shared was the Elliot Clan. In about 1983 Sir Arthur Eliott and Lady Francis Eliott made a tour across Canada from Nova Scotia to British Columbia. Their aim was to set up Clan Chapters in each province. Helen and I drove them to Banff for a dinner at the Banff Springs Hotel and a trip up the gondola. They were somewhat blown away by the beauty of the Rocky Mountains and Sir Arthur was particularly interested in the mountain sheep hanging around the observation platform. We had advertised their presence by both radio and press and held an inaugural meeting in the Army Navy and Air Force building in Montgomery. I ran the meeting, presenting our honoured guests with white hats, while Sir Arthur explained his mission of bringing the worldwide Elliot clan family together. Our Elliot Clan Society of Alberta was incorporated on May 16, 1985 with

Mary Elliott President and yours truly a vice president. I have had several stints as president for Alberta, was national historian for 10 years and appointed to VP for Western Canada, a position I still hold. As Clan historian I have had several papers published both in Canada and internationally.

When Sir Arthur died, he had no male heir and the chieftainship went to his one and only daughter Margaret who is now known as Margaret Eliott of Redheugh. The Elliot Baron title went to some long-lost cousin in the outback of Australia who had no idea he was in line for the Honour and didn't seem to care. When Margaret made her first trip to Canada her first stop was in Vancouver. We attended their meeting and drove Margaret back to Calgary, spending one night in our cottage at Mara Lake. I was still a director of the Calgary flying club and got to use the hanger for our meeting and a good old fashioned western Canadian barbecue. We even put on a square dance demonstration, which Margaret joined in on with great exuberance. Helen and I have attended two of the clan gatherings at Redheugh,

The "Chieftain" and his Lady

Scotland (The ancestral home of the Elliot Clan) and have kept in contact with Margaret by mail. We also joined Margaret at the Halifax International Tattoo when she was honoured as Chieftain of the Day. Unfortunately, all Clan chapters in Western Canada have now closed up shop as we were getting no younger members to take over. Alberta was the last to close our doors in April of this year. I am still VP for Western Canada and we have a few members paying their dues and keeping in touch through the national office in Ontario.

When you get involved in Scottish Clans you automatically tend to drift towards Highland Games, which have been a Keltic tradition since time immemorial. As a Clan we were soon attending Games at Edmonton, Red Deer, Calgary and Canmore. We were the Clan of the Day at Red Deer in 1988 and marched seventy-one Elliotts, or "wannabees" on to centre stage to be honoured – the largest clan representation in Alberta Highland Games history. I got involved with the Calgary Highland Games but was not an official member of CUSGA (Calgary United Scottish Games Association). I was however, their official "Gillie" for several years. A Gillie is the Chieftain of the Day's gopher, golf cart driver and assistant scotch taster – not necessarily in that order. In 2009 I had the great honour of being the Chieftain of the Day. The "K" Division RCMP Pipes and Drums where the duty band that year and were kind enough to "Stack their Drums" and include Helen and I in their official photo.

By then I had my full RCMP tartan regalia, including the only red surge Argyle jacket in Canada. I wore that horse collar Red Serge jacket enough over 26 years and wanted something different. On the advice of two RCMP Band Majors I had an Argyle style jacket tailor made and to my knowledge it is the only one in Canada.

"K" Division RCMP Pipes and Drums

My Time with the Royal Bank

My second career as a credit card crime investigator started in September of 1973 with a three-week learning session at the RBC credit card Centre in Vancouver. My boss was Jack Duggan, a retired RCMP S/Sgt. from British Columbia. We worked together for 12 years until he retired. Unfortunately, as I look back upon that time, I realize that I had too large a territory to cover - BC border to Thunder Bay. It was nice to be my own boss, have an unlimited credit card for expenses and set my own schedule. But it didn't take me too long before I realized that the place I wanted to be was at home with Helen and the boys having wieners and beans. All five major banks had retired RCMP for their fraud investigators and we had a very close bond working together and sharing our intelligence - much to the displeasure of some of the bank managers. For the first three or four years I had to spend three weeks running the Vancouver fraud centre when Jack Duggan took his holidays. He eventually got a second man and shortly after so did I. An RCMP friend Stan Peddie joined me and as he was from Manitoba, he took over Manitoba east and northern Alberta while I kept southern Alberta and Saskatchewan. Credit card fraud investigators were scattered all over North America. We had our own IACCI (International Association of Credit Card Investigators) and I was president of the Prairie Chapter for many years.

Somewhere around 1980 we had our first IACCI International convention in Six Flags Texas. This was located somewhere between Dallas and Fort Worth. Most of the investigators from all banks in Canada attended, together with a few from other countries but the majority were from the United States. It was a bit of an eye opener for us as every session seemed to open with a draw for a weapon of some kind, pistols, rifles, assault weapons, holsters, even knives and ammunition. Of course, you had to be present to win one. It was a little jaw dropping to hear a keynote speaker, the Attorney General for Texas, boast about cutting down on their homicides as they ONLY had 2,700 in all of Texas the previous year. Canada had not experienced that many murders since confederation. The convention lasted all week and we did learn a lot and made a few worthy contacts from around the world. We also got to take in a Dallas Cowboys football game. The best part of it all is that Helen joined me on the weekend, and we spent a couple of nights in Vegas on the way home. It was likely around Easter time as Lee drove Helen to the airport in a blizzard and she arrived carrying her winter coat when the temperature was over 30 degrees celsius. I won a large silver tray at the last night's banquet and then had a hard time getting it through the border on the way home. I don't think we have ever used it as I have a much nicer one given to me by the RCMP Social Committee on my retirement.

For the first few years most of my work was explaining credit cards through seminars held for everyone from judges, prosecutors, police and the merchants who used him. I did frequently track down criminals using stolen credit cards. Unfortunately, most city police would withdraw the fraud charge if the crook pled guilty to some other offences, like breaking and entry or stolen vehicles and then they got credit for solving their cases. Their theory was that the bank had lots of money and could afford the losses, which was not correct as fraud affects everyone. I was slowly able to convince the RCMP, especially the GIS that I could help them if they would help me. With a credit card paper trail I could trace their international crooks all over the world, not only their airplane flights, hotels but even where they ate and how many guests they entertained. In return I got confidential information to help with my inquiries.

The fraud investigators in Toronto covering eastern Canada were either retired Ontario Provincial Police or Toronto city police. They did not have the same connection to confidential information as we RCMP investigators did and they seemed to work only on the major cities. This was exemplified when I tracked down a kid from Nova Scotia who had ridden his motorcycle across Canada and back on stolen credit cards. I turned the file over to our Toronto office, who covered the Maritime's and after several months of waiting they finally admitted they could not get any support from the RCMP. I doubt if they even bothered to try. I looked up the Detachment in Nova Scotia, gave them a call, talked about an Inspector who moved from Calgary down to their area and then brought up my case. The conversation went something like this "I know that bastard and I've been trying to catch him for months. I will look after him." Another case solved. Belonging to a national police force had its advantages.

My work at the bank was not overly rewarding or exciting but the bank did have a lot of perks and one of them was to pay for further education. I decided to fill one more of my desires and signed up for an Adult Ed course at the University of Calgary. I started off with banking and law courses over several winters. One of the papers I prepared was on unions and the banks. This involved all five major banks and mostly concentrated on unpaid overtime and inequities in pay and promotion between the sexes. This not only got me high marks but a very excellent and complementary report from the professor. I turned a copy over to the Personnel Department in the Royal Bank which as far as I know never went anywhere. However, many years later I saw a copy of my work plagiarized almost word for word in the Royal Bank monthly bulletin. There was no mention of Curly Elliott. After completing my 10 courses I graduated with a diploma in Real Estate, which was tucked away in a drawer never to be seen again.

About the time I finished my university courses another challenge came my way with the 1988 Olympics. I was on Eighth Avenue with several hundred other people when the announcement was made that Calgary had won the bid for the Olympics. Within a week I had signed up as a volunteer. I wore many hats over the next four years but was always in the management section. My first job was as security at the 1987 Christmas hockey tournament between Canada and Russia. I was one of the security shift managers with about twenty people scattered around the Saddledome. I soon knew that building from the catwalk to the basement. During the Olympics the main administration and communication centre was on the stampede grounds next to the Saddledome which was too much of a political hub for me. I spent a lot of the three years leading up to the games on orientation - putting volunteers into the right positions and attending more meetings that I had in the previous thirty-five years. By the time the Olympics arrived I had myself established in security working at the opening and closing ceremonies which were held at McMahon Stadium. We also covered the Father David Bauer arena for the hockey games and figure skating practises, with our headquarters in the Olympic speed skating oval. I was one of the four shift supervisors with about fifteen volunteers to look after. We had a few minor incidents but nothing too serious and for the most part it was two weeks of fun and games. I met a lot of nice people from all over the world including a few VIPs – who treated us all with the utmost respect. The two weeks of the Olympics were some of the busiest times in my life, but we also had a lot of fun and I'm glad that I took on this challenge.

Immediately after leaving the Force in 1973 I joined the Calgary Chapter of the RCMP Veterans Association. I was President of our Chapter in 1977/78 and have been actively involved with it now for over forty years. Following on from my service years most of my participation has centred on the social aspect of Chapter activities. That meant working on the committees for three National Annual General Meetings held in Calgary, the last being in 2001 when I was once again the emcee. That was not my last big job as our Veterans financed and commissioned the manufacture of a bronze statue of our second Commr., Colonel James Alexander Farquharson Macleod. He was the one who established Fort Calgary and named the City after his ancestral home in Scotland. The heroic scale (1 1/3 life size) bronze statue was cast using the lost wax method by the Studio West Ltd. Foundry in Cochrane. The owners are Don and Shirley Beggs and Don's dad was one of the ranchers I helped brand with at Butters my first spring in Cochrane. We spent hours researching the historical accuracy of Colonel Macleod's uniform, horse and accoutrements and I was involved in every step of the production. I also contributed considerable financial assistance in our family name towards the completion and erecting of the statute. The Elliott name appears several times on the donor's wall at Fort Calgary.

The unveiling of the Statute was held on September 1st, 2005 Alberta's Centennial Day After the singing of "O Canada" by the Veterans choir, the VIPs guests were piped to the site by three pipers, appropriately wearing the Macleod tartan. The unveiling ribbon was cut by RCMP Commission G. Zaccardelli, while one end of the ribbon was held by James F Macleod, grandson of Col. Macleod and the other by Ken Potts, great grandson of the legendary guide Jerry Potts. The statue was blessed by our Padre, also a veteran and then everyone was piped up to the original fort parade square where a marquee tent and chairs were set up for the VIPs and guests. With everyone comfortable our RCMP Veterans choir, made up of Veterans and their wives, sang the National anthem. I continued on as emcee starting the ceremony by calling upon our veteran cowboy poet Robbie Robertson to relate the history of Colonel Macleod which he did in rhyme. The Commr. gave a passionate address on Colonel Macleod's legacy and how he established a policy of policing with equality, fairness and understanding. He then thanked the Calgary Veterans' Association for their gift to the province, the City of Calgary and the people of Alberta.

Greetings were brought from the various governments, while the judiciary was represented by the Honorable James Laycraft, Chief Justice of the Province of Alberta (retired). James Macleod expressed thanks from that family and their descendants still living in the area. Cecil Crowfoot spoke on behalf of the Treaty Seven Nations. He is the great great grandson of the famous Chief Crowfoot and earned a standing ovation with stories told to him by his grandmother who saw the "Red Coats" arrive on the prairies. The afternoon ended with a fabulous assortment of light refreshments provided by the culinary staff at Fort Calgary and served in the 1888 barracks. This was my last big go at being Emcee and one of the more enjoyable ones. My contributions to the RCMP Veterans were recognized when I was nominated and received one of four Queen's Golden Jubilee medals issued to Calgary Veterans Division. In 2016 I received a Lifetime Certificate of Recognition for my years of volunteer service at Fort Calgary.

Col. Macleod statue as unveiled Sept. 1st, 2005

Don & Shirley Beggs (Bronze sculptors), Gus Buziak (Vet), Me (Vet), Sara Gruetzner (Fort Calgary CEO)

My Fishing Adventures

I was just about to finish my history and realized that I have not included any of my fishing adventures. I am sure if I had overlooked this, Danny would have wanted an appendix. My first fishing trip was at 15 when my two buddies and I spent a few days on an island in the middle of Candle Lake. My last one was in 2015 when Danny, Lee, Brian Montgomery and I spent three days at Ucluelet. That covers about 71 years of fishing so you might say that fishing was in my DNA. I will always remember the last trip as I was recovering from a broken hip and had both Danny and Lee with me. Brian and I have fished together for at least forty years and on more than one trip have been tagged as blood brothers. Lee is not much into fishing, so I was really happy to have him on my last trip and besides that, as the youngest on board he got to be the "official cranker upper" to winch our halibut up from 300 feet or so. We caught lots of fish, told stories, had a few libations and at 86 I was happy to reveal my age and that I was fishing with my two sons.

I didn't fish in the Force until I got to the Peace River area. At High Prairie Cst. Don Kirk and I loaded up a whole gunny sack full of Pickerel, gave them to the Chinese restaurant owner where we ate and had free meals for a month. I think that was my only foray into commercial fishing. When I was stationed in the Valleyview Hotel, my home away from home was with Bob and Kay Keeler who ran a store and holiday resort on Sturgeon Lake. Bob had a commercial license to net White Fish for a 24 hours period each Wednesday. I went out with him once in a while to either help him set or pull his nets. He had an old wooden commercial fish boat with a single cylinder engine that was slow at best and slower when loaded. We started pulling nets one morning and ran into the biggest haul of fish we'd ever seen. Pretty soon our tubs were full, then the floor was covered and before long we were up to our knees with a net and a half still to pull. We finally had to give up on our fish hauling and head back across the lake at a snail's pace. As soon as we got to shore Kay went off to get some Indigenous women to help with the fish cleaning while we unloaded. We went right back to the nets as they had to be out of the water by noon. As expected, the mass of fish ran out within 50 feet and we came back the second time with less than a hundred fish. By mid-afternoon the women had cleaned and iced over a 1000 Lbs. of fish. It was Bob's biggest haul ever and certainly the most fish I ever handled before dinner. I never stayed around to help but went back to the hotel for a bath and a rest. When Helen and I were first married we holidayed free of charge in Keeler's cabins.

When I left the Force and went with RBC, my best friend and colleague was Bill Carter. He was with CIBC, a retired member of the Force and spent all his time in Saskatchewan. Consequently, there was always an inordinate number of fraud cases showing up in the northern Saskatchewan fishing area every spring. We would take a couple of friends with us, stay four or five days and fished all the way from Lac La Ronge to Reindeer Lake. Sometimes we flew in but mostly drove and rented cabins and boats on site. We caught Pickerel, Jack Fish and the odd Lake Trout. Sometimes our catch was a little slim, other times it rained all week, but most of the time it was a lot of fun, fellowship and enjoying the great outdoors. With all those big lakes and us in small boats we lucky to never once get caught in stormy open waters.

Helen and I retired in 1988 and the next year we did our big freedom-from-work trip to Australia, New Zealand and Fiji. We were busing it on the South Island of New Zealand and had a rest day at Queenstown. On the information board was a card advertising a fishing charter. I arranged for a half day trip and next morning I was on Lake Wakatipu with a couple of American honeymooners who knew absolutely nothing about fishing. The guide helped them out while I drove the boat. They caught nothing but I hauled in a nice Rainbow trout. The guide insisted that I take it back to the hotel and that they would cook it for me. I was not buying that - but he talked me into it so I walked into a five star hotel carrying a dead fish by the gills. The girl at the counter shouted "You caught a fish!" to which I replied "Do you want it?" She again assured me that the kitchen would cook it for me so into the kitchen I went. One of the chefs said "Oh you got a fish. How do you want it cooked?" I was so surprised that I said something to the effect that – "You're the Chef you cook it." That night while the rest of our tour got plated food my fish was paraded in with great fanfare and set before me on a fancy decorated fish platter. I also got fish pairing food rather than the standard plated stuff. I can't boast that I have fished all over the world, but that was a memorable day for me, and I've often wondered what would happen if I walked into the Palliser Hotel in Calgary carrying a dead fish for my own supper!!

I fished up and down the Bow River, and in the Shuswap area but after retiring Danny and I have pretty much restricted our fishing to the west coast of BC. We have pretty much covered all the hot spots between the Straits of Juan De Fuca and Alaska. We have fished in every kind of boat from a 14-foot aluminum tub at Sandpit on Haida Gwaii to a 47 foot tri-cabin cruiser out of Prince Rupert. Oddly enough it was from that 14-foot boat that we caught our first 40 lb. salmon and even had two forty pounders on at the same time. We didn't have much room to move around or get excited. For a while we hauled our own boat out to the coast, firstly a 19-foot open aluminum with an outboard and then a 20-foot Reinell cuddy cabin – named Lena Bena, after one of my favourite granddaughters. However, after taking the transmission out of my truck and the engine out of the Reinell and coming home with everything rusted from the sea air – we hit upon a better idea – it is called Pay & Play. We fly to the coast, rent a car and drive across the island to a hotel. In the morning all you have to do is walk to the guide's boat, he finds the fish for you, you catch them, he cleans them and in the evenings all you have to do is eat, drink and tell lies. It does not always work out quite that way, but it is certainly more civilized than bouncing around in an open boat. We have tried fishing lodges once at Knight Inlet and several times at Rivers Inlets. They were nice with good accommodation and food, but you still had to fish on your own in an open boat. I much prefer the bigger boats with a guide who knows what he is doing and where the fish are hanging out at any given time. That's the Play part, when it comes to the Pay you want to have enjoyed the trip as your fish would have been a whole lot cheaper at the Billingsgate Fish Market in Calgary. I have enjoyed most fishing (and hunting) trips and nothing beats being in the great outdoors with your kids and friends.

All fish stories end with the big one that got away and mine are no exceptions. Before Dave went overseas with Shell, he and I were fishing off Port Hardy, BC in my 19-foot aluminum boat. Danny and one of his friends were fishing on the other side of the island in a rental boat. We were after Halibut and of course did not have the right equipment. No such thing as a proper rod and reel for us – we had a 300-pound monofilament line wrapped around a chunk of plywood. When the hook hit the bottom Dave shouted "I got one" – and he sure as hell did! It would move around, but we couldn't get it off the bottom. He finally put the line over his shoulder, bent down and used the full strength of his legs to get the monster moving.

Dave, Danny & I Fishing in Knight Inlet 1985

Lee, me and Danny on my last fishing trip 2015

When we finally got it near the surface and saw how big it was, to say we were excited would be the understatement of the century. It looked like a sheet of plywood and we were doubting if we could even lift it into the boat. In preparation for such an event I had brought along a single shot 22 rifle, but in my excitement, I could not find it and Dave could no longer hold the monster with the line cutting into his hands. We had to do something in a hurry so anchored the line to a cleat on the boat and started looking for a sandy beach to drag it onto. Fortunately, we had him anchored too close to the boat and after a few flips, jumps and rolling around the 300-pound line broke and our Halibut settled slowly out of site. We were steaming mad at the time and I found the 22-rifle wrapped in a plastic bag and tucked under the seat cushions.

When we got in that night and were crying the blues about losing our big fish it didn't take long for the local fishermen, who knew what they were doing to set us straight on how lucky we were that we didn't get our prize into the boat. I have since seen lots of 25 to 50 lb. Halibut boated and those things are a prehistoric monster with a brain the size of a marble. You can beat them over the head with a club for 10 minutes and an hour later they will still jump around and knock things over. Even a 30 pounder should be harpooned or beat to a pulp outside the boat. I am certain that if we had managed to get our BIG FISH into the boat it would have likely injured one or both of us, destroyed the boat and probably made it back into the water. SO, while most fishermen like to brag about their biggest fish ever - I like to tell about the ONE that got away.

Having reached my 88th birthday I must admit I do not have the energy to do all the things that were once routine. Having had several falls last year, I'm also trying to act my age... well, sometimes. I have also given up on much of my volunteering. Ever since I left the bank, I have tried to keep busy helping others in need. For a while I drove cancer patients to the Tom Baker Cancer Clinic for their daytime treatments. I picked them up, drove them to the clinic and then depending on their time of stay either waited for them or came back later to drive them home. I am only twelve minutes from the cancer hospital and since most patients were from the Northwest of the city, I spent more time waiting than driving. I was only doing this a couple of days a week as during the tourist season I was also volunteering at Fort Calgary. I have been a volunteer there for over thirty years. Fort Calgary is not only the birthplace of the RCMP and the City of Calgary but is now a National Heritage site. We acted as ambassadors and regaled the tourists with tales of "The good old days." We also have a number of recycled Red Serge uniforms together with several styles of headgear worn by the Force and we encourage kids and adults alike to put these on and have their pictures taken.

It is a very popular activity, especially with foreign visitors and on a busy day it is not unusual to dress over a hundred people. We have at least nine uniforms of different sizes and when the buses arrive there is always a lineup at our uniform try-on station. I don't do this much anymore but I still show up on special days like May 24th, which of course is both the Queen's and also the RCMP's birthday. I can never seem to be excused on Canada Day July 1st, I am also involved in the November 11th, memorial service. This started out as a little staff and family service and has grown to beyond the capacity of our building. Our RCMP Veteran's Padre is an ex member by the name of Larry Nicolay. He served in BC and upon retiring went to a theology college and is now an Anglican Deacon. He solicited me "for a little help" and now I am running the service, including being emcee, giving the memorial address and supervising the laying of wreaths and poppies. Two years ago, Larry ended up in the hospital and I had to take the full service, including the prayers and benediction. I don't think I'll turn in my red jacket for a backwards clerical collar just yet and have to admit that doing prayers in front of a couple hundred people is a little scary. I am volunteering for the job again this year so I guess I might as well keep on going till I'm at least ninety. One of my other contributions was Red Cross blood donations and in fifty some years I gave over a hundred donations.

In the years leading up to the Olympics Helen was principal at Acadia School and since we were approaching our 60s, total retirement was on both of our minds. Then in May 1977 we had a huge snowstorm and I was in the backyard shovelling snow over my head. Helen fearing I was a candidate for a heart attack decided then and there that it was time for us to move into a condo. Surprisingly enough not long after that Danny announced that one of his friend's parents were selling a condo in Chateaux on the Green Phase II. Helen agreed to work one more year to help with our finances and within a couple of weeks we were the proud owners of our condo in Varsity Estates. Our house at 2411 Uxbridge Dr. NW. sold without too much difficulty and we were in our new home by the end of July 1987. It was the smartest move we've ever made, and condo living has proved to be some of the more relaxed times of our lives. It allowed us to travel extensively with no worries, it's a wonderful neighbourhood and has provided us with nothing but freedom and happiness. Helen has left me in body, but not in spirit, she is still here with all her wonderful art, creativity and her ability to make a house into a loving home. Our sixty-eight years of marriage ended too soon - but not my love for the most beautiful and caring wife to ever marry a farm boy from the bush of northern Saskatchewan.

A Time of Mourning

In the last few years of Helen's earthly journey she was always in pain with an endless series of illnesses. She never once complained and always relied on her quiet inner strength to do things her way. Even when she was diagnosed with breast cancer, she accepted the outcome with quiet dignity and proceeded full steam ahead with the chemotherapy treatment. When she lost all her hair she simply went out and bought a fancy wig to match her own hair and carried on as normally as possible. We managed our final holiday to visit David and Liz in Holland. The four of us then journeyed to Scotland for an "Elliot Clan Gathering" at Redheugh. This was followed by "The Homecoming" of all Scots held in Edinburgh. Scottish descendants from around the world were invited back to Scotland to bring money and attend the Highland Games being held on the grounds of Holyrood Castle. There were 140 Clan tents set up on the grounds and the riot of tartan colours would make a gay pride parade look drab. Helen's enthusiasm was restricted as she was still weak from her surgeries and we were all depressed by Lena's devastating accident. She continued on for several months with her follow up cancer visits and in the spring of 2010 her oncologist assured her that she was 95% cured. He even went so far as to suggest we go on a holiday and have some fun. Helen knew and I suspected that this was not quite the case but being Helen, she would never talk about it. She died in my arms at the Agape Hospice on October 26th, 2010. I have never gotten over losing her, nor will I ever, but life goes on.

About this same time an event took place which I am still not sure I completely understand or have fully accepted. Helen was part of a small unique group of school principals who banded together for mutual assistance. Three of them were Helen, Norreen Baker-Hall (Tom) and Freda Nagy (Joe). Helen, Norreen and Freda were always together at the annual principal's retreat in Fairmount or any time there was a CBE Principals gathering. Joe and Freda Nagy retired to Sorrento, Tom and Norreen holidayed in the Shuswap so the six of us frequently got together in the summer. When Joe and Freda came to Calgary our favourite place for the six of us to dine was the Extreme Restaurant at the entrance to Bowness Park. One day when we both knew that our time together was limited, out of the blue, Helen announced that Norreen's sister Donna was recovering from chemotherapy, had lost her hair and that WE were going to give her Helen's wig. Helen and Norreen talked about Donna but neither of us had met her and she was not in our circle of friends. Arrangements were made for Norreen to pick up the wig and I had to be home to help. Helen was never sneaky in all her life - but she certainly was a schemer and kept her personal thoughts close to her chest. I am left still wondering – was it really the wig or was it a way to bring Norreen and I together? As Ellen Scott (Peggy and Stuart Scott's daughter) put it "Sounds like Norreen was Helen's last gift to you." If so, it was a gift that both changed and saved my life.

Norreen's Tom died two years before Helen and we both supported her during a very difficult period of mourning. Several months after Helen's passing on October 26th, 2010, Norreen, knowing what I was going through, called to see how I was doing. We can't agree on whose idea it was, but we arranged to meet for lunch, and where else but at the Extreme Restaurant. We talked for three hours and it was all about Helen and Tom – Tom and Helen. It was the first time either one of us could expose our vulnerability and have a conversation without breaking into tears. We are now partners living together with a cohabitation agreement and are enjoying life again, it's a new chapter and a new lifestyle. We miss our mates, their names come up every day and while their earthly journeys are over – ours must linger on. In my wildest dreams I never imagined that I would ever, ever have another woman in my life but somehow Norreen has changed all that. Now I'm looking forward to celebrating my ninetieth birthday and maybe a few more.

As I look back in life there are a few things I would have done differently. I would have spent more time at home with Helen and our boys, and a few rough spots could have been avoided, but overall, it has been a long, full and wonderful journey. When I was growing up on a farm, I didn't catch ANY of the usual childhood diseases, even though my older brothers caught them and brought them home. For nearly 70 years after joining the RCMP I lived a healthy life and spent very few days holding down a hospital bed. I did spend a couple of days in Peace River Hospital with a mysterious ailment. However, the wise old doctors soon diagnosed it as, "A Helen Atkins fever" and I was on my way back to Slave Lake. The last ten years have been different, and I can't deny that I am getting older. It seems that my body is not only wearing out and needing repairs, but the indiscretions of my youth are also coming back to haunt me. I have had at least four major surgeries and numerous minor repairs. Sometimes it seems like my only outings are either to the doctor's office or a clinic. What lies ahead and for how long, no one knows, but that's the least of my concerns. Most people don't believe that I am 88, and I answer them with the philosophy I live by: "Age is a number, life is an attitude and every day is a good day." It works for me and I am sticking with it.

Before I close this book, there are many people I must thank for their assistance. I will not mention names as I am sure to miss someone. You all know who you are, and my appreciation is universal. Most of your help has been in my inability to use a computer. Your patience, understanding and tolerances with my computer frustrations have been worthy of an Oscar award. I was ready to quit on more than one occasion and you were there with your kind and gentle assurances that – we can fix it. You copied, flipped, rotated and enhanced my photos, inserting them with skills I could only sit and admire. You found lost chapters and consolidated 15 scattered files into one workable masterpiece. When I was about finished you formatted everything for consistency and appearances giving "our book" its professional look. And, I can't forget my proofreaders who gave me many positive suggestions. They checked every page for composition and spelling, making me proud of a book I am happy to publish on My history and for your enjoyment. Thanks to all of you, for all your generous and gracious help.

PS. "All my stories are tru, becauss I ritt tem myself."
Allan G. Elliott
08-12-2016

My Masonic Lodge and
Concordant Body Affiliations

Year	Notes
1956	Joined Grande Prairie Lodge #105, A.F. & A.M. – July 12th Received Master Masons Degree Sept. 13th, 1956.
1960	Affiliated with King Solomon Lodge # 41, Cochrane, AB
1962	Joined Zenith Chapter #85 Order of Eastern Star (with Helen)
1965	Worshipful Master King Solomon Lodge #41
1969 & 1971	Worthy Patron Zenith Chapter OES #85
1971/72	Provincial Deputy Grand Master District #1
1975	Received and Knighted in the Royal Order of Scotland, Provincial Grand Lodge of Alberta
1976	Helen and I demitted from Zenith Chapter #85. OES.
1977	Joined Calgary Lodge of Perfection Ancient and Accepted Scottish Rite of Freemasonry
1978	Received into Delta Chapter of Rose Croix A & A.S.R. (April 14th) Received into Southern Alberta Consistory A & A.S.R. (Nov. 11th)
1986	Commander-in Chief Southalta Consistory A. & A. S.R.
1998	Coroneted Honorary Inspector General 33-degree A. & A.S.R.
1999	Joined Otuskwan Chapter #9, Royal Arch Masons of Alberta Made Honorary Member of the Royal Order of Scotland, Provincial Grand Lodge of Nova Scotia and Prince Edward Island
2000/05	Alberta Provincial Grand Master, Royal Order of Scotland
2003	Made Knight Companion of the Red Cross of Constantine, Chinook City Conclave #29
2005	Received Appendant Orders of the Holy Sepulcher and St. John the Evangelist, Chinook City Conclave #29 Received Honorary Life Member certificate from Perfection #9
2006	Received fifty Years in Masonry Jewel from Grand Lodge of Alberta
2009	Demitted from all Royal Arch Masons bodies. (Most of my sponsors and friends in Royal Arch Masons had died, late nights were getting hard on me and I wanted to concentrate on my original Lodges.)
2014	Made an Honorary Life Member of King Solomon Lodge #41. (No more dues)
2016	Received Sixty Year bar for my fifty-year jewel, plus a Fifty Year Past Master's Jewel

World Countries and Territories Visited
Throughout a lifetime of Travel
By Curly & Helen Elliott

Year		Country & Trip Notes
1952	1	USA – Honeymoon – North Western States
1973		*RCMP Retirement trip (July/Aug.)*
	2	UK –England, Scotland and Wales
		Fourteen-day eight country European tour
	3	France
	4	Belgium
	5	Holland (Netherlands)
	6	Germany
	7	Switzerland
	8	Liechtenstein
	9	Austria
	10	Italy
1975		Atlantic Provinces with Lee and Aunt Louise
1977		Helen Solo to England with U. of C. Educational tour
1980		San Francisco – for Easter
1981		Hawaii – for Easter
1982		Boston (For Danny and Elizabeth's Wedding) and Nova Scotia
1988		*We both retired and serious touring commenced*
1989	11	Australia
	12	New Zealand
	13	Fiji
1990	14	Mexico (Several years of visiting Jeanie & Dave in Mesa USA)
		Greece and the Holy Land with Craig Tours & Herb O'Driscoll
	15	Greece – Rhodes & Santorini
	16	Israel
	17	Turkey
		Panama Canal Cruise – Acapulco, Mexico to New Orleans, USA
	18	Costa Rica
	19	Panama
	20	San Blas Islands
	21	Venezuela
	22	Grand Caymans

1993		*St. Louis, Branson, Opryland and Graceland with Square Dance tour*

1993   *St. Louis, Branson, Opryland and Graceland with Square Dance tour*
               Orient in Nov. with RCMP Vets. Arranged by Treasurer Tours

     23   Hong Kong
     24   Singapore
     25   Thailand
     26   Malaysia
     27   China

1994   *Western Mediterranean in Oct. with Ed & Ruth Davis Sq. Dance Tour*
               Italy – Rome, Naples, Pompeii, Portofino, & Genoa

     28   Monaco (ship anchored near Nice in France)
     29   Spain – Landed in Barcelona & Ibiza
     30   Gibraltar (U.K)
     31   Morocco – Tangiers
     32   Portugal – disembarked in Lisbon for six-day bus trip

1995   Vets. AGM Whitehorse, Skagway & Salmon fishing

1996   33   Cuba – Two weeks with Marie, Dave, Liz, Jackie and Kimberly

1997   London to Scotland for Elliot Clan gathering at Redheugh, to Holland for
               a week then return to London and bus to Dover for Baltic Cruise on NCL.
               Germany, Kiel Canal & Rostock

     34   Russia – St. Petersburg for 2½ days
     35   Finland –Helsinki
     36   Sweden – Stockholm
     37   Denmark – Copenhagen
     38   Norway – Oslo

1998   Flew to Montreal and back to receive 33º AA&SR, drove through
               Maritimes and returned via Northern USA.
               BC Gulf Islands in Aug. Halifax – funeral for Aunt Louise Custance on
               Sept. 16th Jasper Park Lodge end of Sept. for Alberta A.A.& S.R. 100th,
               anniversary

2000   *Millennium Christmas and News Years with Dave & Liz.*

     39   Canary Islands - Christmas in Tenerife - (Spain)
               New Years in Amsterdam
               Regina RCMP Vets. AGM. Drive back through Black Hills & Mt.
               Rushmore, USA
               Elliott Family Reunion at EmTee Town, Alta.
               Yucatan Peninsula – seven-day tour of Chichen-Itza, Izamal & Uxmal

		Seven days all-inclusive on Mayan Riviera
2002		Fiftieth Wedding Anniversary family Christmas and New Year's cruise
		Western Caribbean: Sailed from Miami, stopping at Cozumel and Grand Cayman Islands
	40	Jamaica – Ocho Rios
2003		Royal Order Meeting in Halifax, RCMP Vets. AGM. Charlottetown, PEI.
		Four Western Province Royal Order Meeting Vancouver
		Edinburgh & Sterling. ROS Grand Lodge meeting
		Christmas and New Year's trip to visit Dave & Liz in Kuala Lumpur, Malaysia
	41	Taiwan
	42	Malaysia - Kuala Lumpur & Fraser Hill – for Christmas
	43	Indonesia – Bali - over New Years
2005		Alaska Cruise on the Holland American Volendam May 18th to 25th
		Elliott Family Reunion at Spruce Holm, Sask. in July
		We sold our Mara Lake Cottage – Bought lot Aug.30, 1972 sold Aug.18 2005
		RCMP Vets. AGM. Halifax, NS. Toured Cape Breton, flew to Dear Lake, toured Northern Peninsula to L'Anse aux Meadows National Park
		Family Eastern Caribbean New year's Cruise on Carnival Triumph
	44	Puerto Rico – San Juan
	45	St. Thomas (USA)
	46	St. Maarten (Netherlands)
		Visited Dave and Liz in Den Haag Holland
	47	Cyprus (Greece) for Easter – Dave & Liz retirement house hunting.
2008		Cypress Hills - Fort Walsh - Saskatchewan. Train trip Settler to Big Valley RCMP Vets AGM in Winnipeg
2009		March spring trip to Victoria - Vets AGM in Whitehorse May 30/31
		Holland with Dave & Liz July 10th, Scotland for Gathering of the Clans July 18th
2010		Helen's cancer returned, our days of travelling stopped, and she died in my arms on October 26th, 2010. Her life ended and for a while so did mine. Fortunately, Norreen Baker, a long-time friend and CBE principal with Helen, entered my world and a new round of travel adventures commenced.
2013	48	Oman - to visit Dave & Liz in Muscat

	49	Qatar - Doha airport only
2014		*South America & Antarctica cruise on HAL Zaandam - Jan. 24th - Feb. 20*
	50	Argentina - Buenos Aires, Iguazu Falls & Ushuaia
	51	Uruguay- Montevideo. Punta del Este
	52	Falkland Islands - Port Stanley
	53	Antarctic Sound - Palmer Archipelago, Drake Passage
	54	Chile – Strait of Magellan, Puerto Chacabuco, Punta Arenas, Castro, Puerto Monti, Valparaiso, Santiago
		Lower Danube River cruise, Budapest to Istanbul
	55	Budapest, Hungary
	56	Vukovar, Croatia
	57	Novi Sad, Serbia
	58	Vidin, Bulgaria
	59	Bucharest, Romania
	60	Istanbul, Turkey
2016		*Newfoundland with Stewart and Louise Elliott*

Manufactured by Amazon.ca
Bolton, ON